MANAGEMENT OF TEACHER EDUCATION

About the Author

G.N. Prakash Srivastava, Reader Regional Institute of Education (NCERT) Bhopal has to his credit books namely *Recent-Trends in Educational Psychology, Personality and Academic Prediction, Recent Approaches to Personality Study, Aadhunik Shiksha Manovighyan, Vikas Manovighyan Evam Shiksha* and *Advanced Research Methodology*. Apart from these he had been co-author of *Child Understanding and Development, Handbook of Social Science Teaching* (NCERT), and *Indian Girls.* More than 75 papers and 15 monographs, 5 MHRD Projects and ERIC (NCERT) Project (on Restructuring Internship in Teaching) are also his significant contributions. His MHRD, Government of India sponsored visit to Israel brought forth a unique report on the Education of the Gifted Children. He has guided more than three dozen post-graduate and doctorate research students. At present he is completing D.Litt. in Education on 'Present Scenario and Perspective Model of Teacher Training in India'. As an eminent scholar, his name has been included in "Learned Asia", "Indo-European: Who's Who", Who's Who is Indo-American Education", and "Reference Asia: Who's Who of Men and Women of Achievement". He had been Secretary of UNESCO sponsored project on the Teacher Training for Disadvantaged Children. His contribution in a number of National and International Seminars gathered much appreciation. Researches in the field of Personality, Motivation, Internship and Academic Achievement with Prediction Equations are some other unique contribution to his credit. The American Biological Institute U.S.A. has conferred on him the decree of "Man of the Year, 1998". "Who's Who of the year 1999', and 'Outstanding Man of the 20th century', for his outstanding contribution.

MANAGEMENT OF TEACHER EDUCATION A HANDBOOK

G. N. Prakash Srivastava
Reader, Regional Institute of Education (NCERT), Bhopal

CONCEPT PUBLISHING COMPANY, NEW DELHI-110059

ISBN : 81-7022-810-7 (H.B.)

First Published 2000

Published and Printed by
Ashok Kumar Mittal
Concept Publishing Company
A/15-16, Commercial Block, Mohan Garden
New Delhi-110059 (INDIA)
Phone : 5648039, 5649024
Fax : 091-11-5648053

PREFACE

Teacher Training Programme has travelled a long way from Herbartian system to Micro Teaching, Mini Teaching, Models of Teaching and now to School Experience Programme (SEP). Taking birth in Medical Science Internship in Teaching landed in India from United States. It flourished in NCERT through Regional Colleges of Education in the sixties, counteracted with the wave of Micro Teaching and Interaction Analysis in the seventies and subsided with Models of Teaching.

Approaches to the development of professional skills and competencies in preservice teachers revolve around the provision of guided experience in school or school like situations. Almost universally this involves the placement of student teachers in actual schools and classrooms for varying periods of time and at varying stages in their preparation. Practice teaching aims to develop in students (trainee-teachers) a habit of scepticism and inquiry not just in regard to pedagogical practices but also in their appraisal of the institutions in which they teach. Secondary Teacher Education Curriculum Guidelines and Syllabi (NCERT, 1991) introduced a new nomenclature 'School Experience Programme (SEP)' to it.

The present volume is an attempt to provide guidelines for organising Internship, Practice Teaching and School Experience Programme. It may prove a very useful tool in the hands of teacher-educators and teacher-trainees in the completion of practicum in teacher education programme. It consists of all the practical steps from pre-internship, core-training skills to the post-internship activities along with the necessary formats for lesson-planning, assignments, supervision, and evaluation of teaching-competencies etc. The terms "student-teacher," "teacher-trainee", "beginning-teacher", "prospective-teacher", "intern", and "apprentice teacher" etc. have been used synonymously in this volume.

Teacher-training institutions including IASEs, CTEs, University Departments of Education in India may manage their teacher-training programme with the help of guidelines provided in this volume. It is one of the most comprehensive document developed so far in the field of teacher preparation.

May 22, 1999 G.N. PRAKASH SRIVASTAVA

ACKNOWLEDGEMENTS

The present volume is an outcome of my experiences in the field of Teacher Education for about three decades first at Banaras Hindu University and then at Regional College/Institute of Education (NCERT) Bhopal. It is the result of the review of numerous literature on teacher education both Indian and foreign along with my personal experience and research on teacher training. I am thankful to all the thinkers, educationists, teacher educators, and researchers whose findings have been incorporated in this handbook. I am also grateful to my teachers and colleagues who supported me in this venture directly or indirectly. Being Incharge of Internship in Teaching Programme a R.I.E. Bhopal for about one decade I became increasingly interested to develop such a handbook for teacher preparation in the absence of which many teacher training institutions face difficulties in providing suitable guidance and supervision to teacher trainees.

My hearty thanks goes to Shri Arun Gupta, Ajay Publishers and Distributors, Bhopal who has always been a source of inspiration and motivation to my creative endeavour. His cooperation in the publication and circulation of my books deserve special appreciation.

May 22, 1999 G.N. PRAKASH SRIVASTAVA

CONTENTS

1

INTRODUCTION

"Teaching" denotes action undertaken with the intention of bringing about learning in another. In this way, teaching is different from mere telling or showing how. Thus there is some encounter between the teacher and the student, the teacher intends what he or she does to contribute to the student(s), and the actions are reasonably conducive to bringing the student(s) learning. This means that normally teaching acts fall within a range of activities that includes explaining, describing, demonstrating, exemplifying, guiding etc.

"Training" is used in a pejorative way less frequently than either "conditioning' or "indoctrination" and accordingly, has more substantial area of overlap with "educative teaching". In many contexts "teaching" can be substituted for "training". The focus of training is on the development of skills, on knowing—how rather than knowing—that. Some times "training" is reserved for use in the context of teaching of routine tasks which allow total mastery, but this is by no means always the case. Teaching someone a skill requires developing the learner's capacity to respond to the unexpected, to understand what he or she is doing and why, to be intelligent and reflective in the exercise of his/her skill. Such teaching, therefore, involves the giving of reasons rather than (or in addition to) drill.

Practice teaching is one of a variety of terms applied to that part of a student teacher's professional training that involves the student in trying to teach pupils. Practice normally takes place in school and although arrangements are sometimes made for students to teach pupils in college, the use of the term practice teaching implies that activity takes place in schools. Other terms used more or less synonymously are teaching practice, school experience, student teaching, field experience, and practicum. In teacher-training institutions practice teaching forms a major component in the course of training.

In the practice teaching component of most training courses, student teachers engaged in practice teaching spend several weeks in schools practising to teach pupils. They are guided by tutors/college supervisors of the training institutions and by cooperating teachers. The guidance mostly consists of discussion prior to teaching, occasional observation by tutor or cooperating teachers of the student teaching, and a post-teaching discussion when the tutor or cooperating teacher comments on the student's performance. The guidance that is given is rarely related to any body of pedagogical principles and mostly consists of practical advice from a corpus of crafts know-how developed over time by teachers. Practice teaching is therefore seen as providing opportunities to display, recognise, and refine the abilities that are latent in the student. If practice teaching is the single most powerful intervention in a teacher's professional preparation, then the supervision of the student teacher is the single most powerful process in such intervention.

Teacher Training

Practice Teaching and Internship

The development of the normal school in the early 19th century included the apprenticeship approach in the teacher education curriculum. The approach was largely that of "Practising" the teacher acts. The "Practice Teaching" concept lingered for many years, through the teachers' college era into schools of education in multipurpose institutions. Practice teaching was based on the premise that the prospective teacher was first taught the theory and then introduced to the classroom teaching to practice that theory.

The philosophy persisted until the middle of twentieth century in the advanced countries and then the practice teaching approach changed along with terminology of the experience. "Practice Teaching" gave way to "Student Teaching" in which the prospective teacher was considered to be a student of teaching during the classroom experience. The changed philosophy resulted from the realization that teachers could not be educated away from the realities of the classroom and that theory could be assimilated only as it was put into action. Thus theory was related to teaching and learning in a more meaningful way. With proper help and guidance from the supervisory personnel who would work with him the student teacher would expand and develop his understanding of teaching.

The position of "Cooperating teacher" gave the teacher opportunity to ply his trade—another opportunity to teach. The use of video cameras enabled the student teacher to see himself at work in the classroom, and the addition of interaction analysis techniques made it possible to quantify the process of teaching into the identifiable categories. The entire supervisory process rapidly became more analytical in its approach.

It became obvious that if he were to attain the new goals of student teaching, the prospective teacher required a longer, more varied, and more extensive classroom experience. This led to the move from the college campus to the public schools, where longer assignments were possible.

As currently used the term "teaching practice" has three major connotations: the practicing of teaching skills and acquisition of the role of a teacher; the whole range of experience that students go through in schools; and the practical aspects of the course as distinct from theoretical studies.

Objectives of Student Teaching/Practice Teaching

The shift toward the more analytical approach to student teaching has resulted in a change in objectives. No longer is student teaching expected to result in mere tricks of the trade; the objectives are more global in nature. Hilliard and Durrance (1968) listed the objectives of student teaching as under:

The student teaching experience, if it occurs in a clinical climate, does provide valuable means for guiding the student teacher's growth through a carefully planned sequence of activities which enable him to—

- Clarify his understanding of the purposes, development, programmes, and administrative organization of education.
- Broaden his understanding of curricular practices.
- Deepen his understandings of the principles of human growth and development and the learning process.
- Become sensitive to the social patterns of a school community and discover through first hand experiences ways of improving curriculum for pupils by effective use of community resources.
- Develop wholesome professional attitudes towards members of the teaching profession.
- Identify his strong points and weak points in the wide spectrum

of competencies associated with effective teaching.
— Become increasingly resourceful and creative in planning, developing, and evaluating effective learning experience for and with pupils.

Another statement of the objectives of student teaching which typifies the change in objectives is that of Indiana University. This statement is illustrative of aims listed by many teacher-preparating institutions in their handbooks written for cooperating teachers. The Indiana University statement suggests that the student teaching experience should attempt:

— To provided for professional development of young teachers through integration of theory and practice.
— To help students achieve a realistic understanding of the individual child as a developing human being.
— To help the student see more clearly the relationship of the school with the community it serves.
— To promote the growth of student-teachers by encouraging them to read and to become familiar with professional books, magazines, resources units, audio-visual aids, and other materials related to their teaching experiences.
— To guide the beginning teacher in understanding the total organization of the modern school.
— To develop certain important abilities involved in planning teaching-learning activities; in organizing materials of instruction to provide for the individual needs, interests, and capacities of youth; in handling routine elements of classroom management; and in evaluating pupils' educational growth.
— To continue the development of essential personality characteristics of teachers such as breadth of interest, curiosity, dependability, and cooperation.

In the Bristol study, Brimer and Cope (1971) analysed the objectives of practice teaching as perceived by students staff and teachers in the practice schools of colleges of education as follows:

— To provide the student with an opportunity to establish an appropriate teacher-pupil relationship with children.
— To provide the student with an opportunity for applying theory

to be applied in the practical situation and to assist him, where necessary, to discriminate between inappropriate theory and the inadequate implementing of sound theory.

— To provide an opportunity for evaluating the student's potential as a teacher and suitability for the teaching profession.
— To provide the student with an experience of success in the teaching situation so that the student acquires confidence.
— To provide an opportunity in the practical teaching situations for the extension and deepening of the student's self-knowledge.
— To provide the student with practical experience in schools which will reveal some of the problems of discipline and enable him to develop personal methods of control.
— To provide the student with opportunities for developing ability of organization.
— To provide an opportunity for the student to develop and display qualities of adaptability and sensitivity appropriate to the school situation.
— To provide the student with an opportunity of becoming part of the school community, familiarizing himself with its practices and entering into appropriate professional relationships with its adult members, the most significant of which is his relationship with the class or subject teacher.
— To provide for the interchange of ideas and methods between schools and college by college staff and students perceiving new ideas, materials and equipment in use in schools, and by college staff and students introducing new ideas, materials and equipment into schools.

Perhaps the most important outcome for student teachers is a personal one—the development of self-confidence and a sense of security to the point where he can enter his first teaching position with a feeling of competence. This self-confidence is the result of the many varied activities in which the student teacher participates in the well-planned and well-developed practice teaching programme.

Significant outcome of the student teaching experience is the creation of an awareness of what constitutes good teaching and the readiness of the student teacher habits. Another objective usually met in student teaching is reorganization of subject matter in the mind of the student-teacher. Although it must also be recognized that many student-teachers learn new content during student teaching, the major attainment in this area is the modification of content previously learned into the structure of the school curriculum and along the lines of the understanding that the pupils possess. Along with this modification is acquaintance and familiarization with the many types of teaching materials available and appropriate for use with pupils at the level for which the student-teacher is preparing to teach.

Finally it is reported by student teachers that one of the most valuable outcomes of the student-teaching-experience is a much better understanding of boys and girls. The perspective of the teacher toward the pupils is a new for the college student, and, as a result, the prospective teacher gets new insights into the emotional, physical, mental and social aspects of the children and youth with whom he comes in contact.

The good student-teaching programme is clinical in nature. The various activities in which the student-teacher participates must be carefully prescribed, diagnosed, and analyzed so that the prospective teacher may better understand the reasons for his success and failure and many become acquainted with alternatives.

Terminology

Although the vocabulary of student-teaching is fairly standardized, frequent misunderstandings emerge. The dynamic status of student-teaching and other clinical experiences at present lead to new terms, changing definitions, and semantic difficulties. In order to facilitate understanding and to avoid misconceptions, the following definitions are those which will be followed in the ensuing pages.

Co-operating Teacher

The classroom teacher in the schools who is given the responsibility of working directly with a student-teacher. Synonymous of this term is "supervising teacher," although past usage reserved this title for teachers who work with student-teachers in the laboratory school. The cooperating teacher designation more easily differentiates this position from that of the college supervisor.

College Supervisor

The designated faculty member of the teacher-education-institution who has the responsibility for supervising a number of student-teaches in various school assignments. He also provides consultant services to the student-teacher and the cooperating teacher and serves in a liaison capacity between the schools and the college in matters concerning student-teaching. Other terms used interchangeably with college supervisor are "university supervisor" or "campus supervisor" and "college coordinator". In a few cases, this role is played by persons jointly appointed by the college and the schools.

Student Teaching

Classroom teaching is one of the experiences provided to many prospective teachers. It is a period of guided teaching during which the student takes increasing responsibility for the instruction of a given group of learners over an extended period of time. The experience is usually provided under the direct supervision of a classroom cooperating teacher or the University/College Supervisor.

Internship

Internship is an integral part of professional preparation of a teacher in making preceded by successful observation—participation and student teaching or equivalent clinical experiences in a school environment, and is planned and coordinated by the teacher education institution in cooperation with one or more school systems. Intern in a prospective teacher who assumes an internship position in which he is given a teaching position under guidance. Often he is involved in accompanying professional courses simultaneously with his teaching duties.

Internship is service in preparation for a position usually under the supervision of a university or college and a practicing school teacher more experienced in the field. It consists of wide variety of experiences undertaken in one or more schools. The Intern is given opportunity to participate in many phases of the work of the school system. Frequently his practical work in the school system is correlated with further work at, and/or guided by the teacher training institution.

The Internship in teaching is to lead teacher-trainees to the culminating point in his field experiences which comprise both observation and participation in the different activities of the school. It envisages the student working over continuous period of time with the staff of a school and performing the roles expected of a new ideal teacher. A distinctive term has been given to this arrangement to distinguish it from the usual practice teaching by the fact that the student is initiated to first hand experiences as a teacher.

The Plan and Programme (NCERT, 1963) mentions, "The term Internship" refers to an arrangement under which a prospective teacher can acquire first hand experience as a teacher in situations closely resembling those in which he would be working upon entering the profession. The Internship Programme is to be so designed as to provide each student with a comprehensive experience and will be implemented in realistic teaching learning situation in the cooperating schools. To make the total experience similar to actual teaching student will work full time in the cooperating schools in a block of about eight weeks.

Page and Thomas (1977) in the International Dictionary of Education consider internship as "probationary period served by newly qualified teachers. According to these authors the holder of an Internship Programme is known as an intern. Internship may be in lieu of student teaching, yet the dictionary equivalent is probationary year." As a supplement to the conventional student teaching programme, internship offers a means for greater involvement in teaching, makes for more assumption of responsibility, and puts the prospective teacher in professional role as he completes his preparation programme.

As a vehicle for teacher education and certification, the internship can be traced to the early years of the present century, although many persons are inclined to consider the internship in teacher education as a new departure in teacher preparation. Milestones in the development of the internship concept are the Brown University programme which began in 1909, the cooperative programme of the University of Cincinnati and Cincinnati Public Schools in 1919, the expansion of internship programmes during depression years of the 1930s, and the importance provided by private foundations in the late 1950s and throughout the 1960s. In spite of this fairly long historical background, however, the internship has yet to become a significant factor in the mass production of teachers.

There are those who apparently feel that all teacher education should move toward the internship concept. Many authorities, however, feel that the internship should be reserved for carefully selected and especially prepared persons since the teaching assignments assumed by these persons enlist much more responsibility and instructional duties than student teachers assume. When one considers that the intern fills the same position as a fully certificated teacher, it becomes obvious that he must be somewhat more proficient than the usual teacher candidate for shouldering his professional responsibilities. It is highly probable, however, that internship programmes will continue to increase in number and that more and more teachers will be produced in this manner.

The recognition of the need for pre-internship teaching experiences has led to some interesting variations for providing clinical involvements. Some Training Institutions use the micro-teaching technique to provide teaching expertise for its interns. Some institutions created special summer schools in which interns did a modified student-teaching assignment. Still other colleges and universities employed simulation techniques for this purpose. There are some institutions, of course, which utilize a conventional student-teaching experience prior to the internship assignment.

Internship programmes may be found at both the elementary and secondary levels. However, teacher education programmes appear to rely on the internship approach more at the secondary teacher preparation level. Correspondingly more graduate programmes appear to be at the secondary level while more of the undergraduate programmes appear to be elementary in orientation.

Characteristics of Internship Programme

The internship differs from conventional student-teaching in many ways, yet there are similarities: the prospective teacher becomes involved in teaching; supervision is provided by both the college and the schools; self-evaluation and clinical analysis is an integral part of the process. The differences that are most obvious have to do with the amount of responsibility given to the perspective teacher, the nature of the supervision, and in some instances the length of the teaching assignment.

The intern normally assumes the major responsibility for the instruction of a group of learners for an extended period of time. He is usually immersed in teaching from the outset of his assignment and does not have the luxury of the gradual involvement which is found in many student teaching assignments. While supervision is provided to him it is not as readily nor as easily available as may be found in most student teaching programmes.

The college supervisor in internship programmes frequently assumes more of a consultant role than is found in student-teaching. Other than this the role is comparable to that in student-teaching programmes. Supervision from the public schools may be found in various patterns. Usually there is a classroom teacher who is released from other teaching duties to assume the responsibility of working with a small number of interns.

The differences that exist among internship programmes include the level of instruction (graduate or undergraduate), the college degree earned, the amount of actual actual teaching, the time of the teaching assignment with respect to other professional courses, and the overall structure of the internship programmes.

In many programmes, academic or professional courses are taken concurrently with the internship teaching experience. This is sometimes necessary in order that the required courses be covered within the short period of time available. Such practice is questionable since the intern usually has all he can handle effectively in his teaching assignment alone. This has been reported as a consistent problem and a concern of graduates for internship programmes.

After carefully analysing fourteen representative internship programmes, Dorothy Blackmore (1968) reported the following generalisations concerning the characteristics of the programmes studied.

— Theory courses are usually given concurrently with, and in connection with, pre-internship laboratory experiences of a practical nature. These courses and the related field experience are ordinarily planned, coordinated and taught by people involved in the practical phase of the internship laboratory experiences in preparation for internship teaching.

— Both theoretical course work and problem—centered seminars generally accompany the internship in teaching during its entirety.

— Micro-teaching and video taping are extensively used in internship programmes as means of providing feedback on teacher behaviour. These are frequently accompanied by the use of a clinical instrument or theoretical guide for analysis of classroom interaction and as means of changing or improving the teaching activity.

— Extensive personalised, supervision is an important feature of all programmes studied. In fact, most reports indicate that the supervisor, highly skilled in the interpretation of theory to the intern, is the key of the intern's successful implementation of theory in the classroom.

— Internship generally seems to be conceived as a programme requiring the interaction of many different individuals in varying professional roles rather than as a function of education departments alone. Commonly involved are both theoreticians and practitioners at a number of levels. . .

— Finally, coordination and cooperation among all the agencies involved are felt to be necessary to bring about the most effective integration of theory and practice in internship.

Internship programmes are also characterised by identifiable stages through which the interns pass as they approach the full realization of their professional goal. These stages are not dissimilar to those earlier identifiied for student teachers, except for the addition of shock realization which occurs early in the assignment.

The Supervision of Interns

The supervisor, frequently called the intern consultant, has a different role to play from that of the student teaching supervision teacher; the relationship, the control, and the instructional framework differ considerably from that of the conventional student teaching assignment. John Chaltas (1968) and colleagues suggest that the one basic ingredient in internship supervision which is lacking in student teaching is autonomy. Obviously, the intern is not completely autonomous in his classroom instruction, but he does have considerably more freedom in making choices and decisions, in planning his approaches, and in determining content than does his student teaching counterpart.

In the internship structure the interm is not dependent upon the supervisory personnel to tell him what to teach and when to teach it. He has a different relationship—that of a fellow teacher. The intern consultant is just that—a consultant with respect to suggesting ways for the improvement of instruction.

The kind of person selected for the supervisory consultant role should have characteristics similar to that of the cooperating teacher in student teaching programmes except that frequently more experience is required. The intern consultant often works with interns who teach at different grade levels and in different subjects rather than in the limited, self-contained, narrow subject area in which student teachers usually work. Normally the supervisory situation is improved if the consultant has had experience in those subjects and at those levels with which the interns under his supervision are involved. Other than this the same qualities of desiring good human relationships, courtesy, understanding of instructional problems, the ability to analyse and diagnose teaching activities, and the realization of the values of careful evaluation are desirable for both kinds of supervisory roles.

Consultant personnel should make regular and frequent visits to intern teachers, always encouraging them to ask questions, to voice concerns, and to raise issues in which they need help. If possible. One of the problems in this respect, of course, is to overcome the stigma created by many supervisory practices of the past.

Advantages of Internship Programmes

Those who work in internship programmes emphasize that their trainees appear to be better prepared than those produced by more conventional teacher education programmes. There is an added emphasis on clinical experiences in the internship.

Interns appear to be as well prepared as those of conventional programmes. Additionally there is considerable evidence that those who enter the teaching profession through the internship route remain in teaching as a career for a longer period of time than those who enter through conventional channels. This is hardly surprising in view of the fact that those who go through internship usually have a greater investment in their professional preparation and make the decision to enter teaching, in many cases, after graduation from college at a time when they are more certain of their goals and are more sure of themselves in the selection of teaching as career (Bennie, 1972).

In Indian Context

Internship in teaching as visualised in the Plan and Programme (NCERT 1963) for which an alternative terminology "School Experience Programme" (SEP) has also been used by Secondary Teacher Education Curriculum (NCERT, 1991) is to be designed to provide opportunities to develop high level of competence in all aspects of the teacher's work. During this period, the student teachers have to work full time in the cooperative schools. They are to be provided with a wide variety of experiences, designed to develop teaching competency such as working with individual students, guiding students, group practice teaching and evaluating students' progress. This has also to provide trainees ample opportunities to acquaint themselves with the school and community and the usual functions of a school. The duties and responsibilities of the teacher of today take him for beyond the limits of the class work.

Classroom teaching skill is not the only requirement of a good and effective teacher. The teacher training colleges have also to provide experiences in the co-curricular activities, effective library service, organization of physical games and sports, guidance in choice of courses and careers, reporting students progress, maintenance of record and registers and even aspects like planning for purchase of equipment and apparatus for the laboratory. All these require training and experience for professional efficiency as a teacher. Internship in teaching has to provide the student-teacher an opportunity to acquire all necessary skills for the profession.

Organising Internship

Because of the importance of Internship in the total programme of the teacher-training course, as well as the complexities of Internship, organising Internship calls for a great care and deftness on the part of the organisers of Internship. Organisation of Internship involves the important stages—selections of Internship centres, arranging Pre-Internship Conference, conduct of Internship and Evaluation. Each stage is crucial for the success of Internship. We now turn to examine these stages in some details.

Pre-Internship Programme

Selection of Internship Centres

The first step in organising Internship is to select the schools for the conduct of Internship for our trainees. The selected schools will be called the Co-operating Schools and the heads and teachers of these schools are the Cooperating Heads and Teachers respectively.

Selection of Co-operating Schools

The Cooperating Schools should be selected on the basis of the following criteria:

— Reputation of the school and its willingness to use new and improved teaching techniques. This is to be based on the recommendations of the state departments of education, extension service centres, inspectors, headmasters, college staff-members and professional organisation.

— The training, experience and competence of the teachers in the special departments selected.
— The availability of adequate physical facilities in the schools.
— High degree of interest, enthusiasm and ability to participate in programme on the part of the school management, headmaster and the staff.
— Breadth and quality of the total programme of the school.
— Location of the school in order to meet the needs of the student-teachers who come from a wide geographic area.
— Medium of instruction in the school (medium in which trainees will require to teach).
— The provision of suitable housing arrangements for student-teachers.
— Availability of adequate classes for the interns to teach.
— Those which can provide students teachers in shaping them to be good teachers.

The State Education Department should issue a circular to all the schools to provide a willing co-operation to Internship in Teaching Programme for discharging their roles and responsibilities as co-operating schools.

Schools that are suitable for the internship are approached to obtain their willingness, to help in internship. Having secured the willingness, the formalities of getting permission by the concerned educational authorities of the schools are attended to by the college. With such a permission the cooperating schools are selected and the same is intimated to the schools formally by the college.

Pre-Internship Meeting

For The Student-Teachers/Interns

In order to brief the student-teachers who are proceeding for Internship about the Internship arrangements and the expectations from them, a Pre-Internship meet is arranged. During this meet, the student-teachers know their duties and responsibilities at their Internship centres besides information regarding the centres. Their attention is drawn to the following points:

(a) teaching responsibilities—the quantum of teaching (interns of periods) they are required to do.

(b) the materials they can get from the centres and those they need to carry with them (as kits chemicals, books, etc.)

(c) the co-curricular and extra-curricular activities they can do at the centres.

(d) the research projects they can undertake.

(e) the community work they can undertake.

(f) the rules and regulations of the co-operating schools and the dos and donts that they need to observe, strictly.

(g) the records to be maintained by them for evaluation purpose.

Besides the last minute briefing, they are supplied with necessary forms as the Teaching Profile, Student-Teachers Diary, Lesson-Observation Format, list of records to be maintained, etc.

Conferences of Cooperating Heads/Principals and Teachers

A Pre-Internship Conference is conduct prior to the commencement of internship in which the cooperating heads and teachers participate to know about the college in general and about the way the college would like the internship to be in particular. It is an opportunity for the college faculty as well to meet the cooperating heads and teachers to know about the schools in turn. Thus it is mutually beneficial. Through lectures, lecture-cum-discussions and demonstration lessions, different aspects of internship are presented and analysed. Here opinions on different aspects of internship are discussed and clarified such a dissemination goes for in making the internship more meaningful.

The discussions center around:

(a) Meaning and scope of internship.

(b) Planning lesson on different aspects.

(c) Objectives based teaching.

(d) Evaluation in teaching.

(e) Evaluation of lessons (use of the teaching profile).

(f) Activities during internship besides teaching.

(g) Role of cooperating heads and teachers in internship.

The cooperating heads and teachers will enlighten the student-teachers and the faculty members of the college about their schools during the centre-wise meetings.

Pre-Internship Orientation/Readiness Activities

Before the interns are placed in the Cooperating Schools for practice-teaching and Internship Activities, a Pre-Internship Orientation Programme should be organised atleast for six weeks. The planning and organisation of the programme should be done in a democratic way, seeking the help of school teachers, student-teachers and teacher-educators.

The following activities may be taken by under the orientation programme:

* Orientation of college supervisors, cooperating teachers and principals for their supervisory roles and other responsibilities in the proper implementation of Internship programme.
* Organisation of Headmasters or Principals conference.
* Orientation of Interns for their field assignments and Projects to be completed during Internship.
* Visits to schools to study the school environment and pupils, to observe teachers at work and various activities of the schools.
* Discussion on the observed lessons of school teachers.
* Training in observation schedule to develop observation skills indicating what, how, when and why to observe and also to write a concise report on observation of lessons during practice-teaching.
* Training is core-teaching skills such as:

  — Skills of Class Management
  — Skills of communication which may include (i) Narration, (ii) Recitation, (iii) Dramatisation, (iv) Explanation and (v) Demonstration.
  — Skills of Interaction (Teacher-Pupils Acts) which may include (i) Questioning and Feedback, (ii) Discussion, (iii) Problem-Solving.
  — Skills for use of Teaching Aids under which training should be provided on:

    (i) Selection of Teaching aids.
    (ii) Preparation of charts, models, maps and diagrams.
    (iii) Operation of mechanical aids.
    (iv) Positioning while writing on and explaining from the blackboard.

(v) Writing on the blackboard with reference to size, shape, boldness and colour of letter.

(vi) Drawing, sketching, preparing tables and graphs on the blackboard.

— Skill of Reinforcement and control including positive and negative reinforcement, verbal and non-verbal reinforcement, encouragement, cuing and silence.
— Skill of Questioning, elaborating, introductory questions, spread of questions to all members of the class, developing questions, thought-provoking questions, probing questions, higher-order questions, recapitulatory questions and the framing of questions.
— Skill of illustrating with examples.
— Skill of stimulus variation.

* Delivering lessons in simulated conditions.
* Organisation of Demonstration Lessons and holding discussions on them.
* Orientation on child psychology and teaching-learning process.
* Orientation on techniques of motivation and inspiration for learning.
* Training in Guidance and counselling techniques.
* Training in organising activities and discussion sessions.
* Training and Practices in Lesson-Planning, Unit-Planning and Lession-Notes.
* Orientation about the use of facilities available in schools.
* Practice in at least one model of teaching.
* Orientation on various methods of teaching.
* Training in preparation of Achievement tests and Diagnostic-tests.
* Training in Role-Play, Brain-storming and Dramatisation.
* Providing related materials to Interns.
* Orientation on:

— Textbook analysis.
— Remedial teaching
— Formulation of objectives
— Organisation of Parent Teacher Association.
— Case study, lab. study and school plant study.
— Study of school records, Admission, Procedure, Registers,

Preparation of result, Fee collection and records.
— Organisation of School Activities/Co-curricular Activities.
— Class-work and Home work.
— Preparation of time-table, school-calendar and cumulative records.

Internship Activities

The Internship activities should include:

* Placement of Interns in the Cooperating schools keeping in view the sufficient facilities and classes available in various subjects to be taught by Interns.
* Proper acquaintance of trainee with the school.
* Fixing time-table for Interns and allotment of units to be taught by Interns.
* Preparation of Lesson Plans by Interns and getting them corrected by subject teachers and teacher educators.
* Practice-Teaching by Interns and supervision and feedback by supervisor and cooperating teacher.
* Participation in group discussion by the Interns, Cooperating teachers and college supervisor.
* Observation of lessons of seasoned teachers by Interns.
* Preparation of appropriate teaching aids by Interns.
* Designing the unit tests, administering them, evaluating and providing feedback to students by Interns.
* Preparation of progress-reports or progress-cards.
* Interaction with parent (of students) during Teacher-Parent Meet.
* Organising subject quiz.
* Organizing subject exhibitions.
* Participation in subject-clubs and promoting other school activities.
* Observation of peers on practice lessons. Lessons by interns on the observation schedule.
* Completion of field-assignment by the Interns under the guidance and supervision by the supervisors.
* Guidance by supervisors in class-management, preparation and use of teaching-learning aids.
* Meeting with the cooperating school Principal, teachers and

school functionaries and discussion with them on the Internship Programme.

* Organisation of Co-curricular activities in the school under the supervision of school teachers and supervisors.
* Participation in working with community programme to know the community and its problem and try to help in solving these problems.
* Experience in Library, laboratory and record maintenance.
* Completion and report on some action research.
* Making case studies and preparation of report of at least two case studies of problem children/gifted children/retarded children.
* Analysis of Textbooks and question papers.
* Lab. study and school plant study.
* Preparation of school calendar.
* Study and preparation of school registers and other documents such as fee book, admission forms and admission register, attendance registers, transfer certificate, stock register etc.
* Assessment of the use of library by the students.
* Study of the school environment and its socio-cultural fabric.
* Visit to various places of educational significance, such as:

  — Rural-craft centres, farms, cottage industries etc.
  — Juvenile courts, remand homes etc.
  — Special schools for the handicapped.
  — Visit to historical places, monuments, museums, industrial units and geographical places etc.

Post-Internship Activities: They Include:

— Post internship Meeting of Interns and supervisors.
— Evaluation of Assignments.
— Viva-voce on Internship Experiences.
— Exhibition of Teaching Aids prepared by Interns.
— Post-Internship Seminars and Discussions.
— Inviting feedback from school authorities.
— Preparation of brief report by each Intern about his/her Experience during Internship alongwith the suggestions for improvement.
— Submission of the report of peer-group supervision.
— Suggestions by Interns, School-teachers and supervisors for strengthening Internship Programme.

2

TRAINING IN TEACHING SKILLS

Core Teaching Skills

Before the placement of trainees in the cooperating schools for Teaching Practice/SEP/Internship they are to be trained in certain Core-Teaching Skills. In many teacher-training institutions it is known as Micro Teaching. NCERT (1979) in the "Organisation of Core Training Programme package" has also identified some skills for teacher training. Micro Teaching Approach has its own long list of teaching skills and models of Teaching Approach has its own strategies and procedures. An attempt is made here to evolve a feasible, practical and useful model of Training in Core Teaching Skills. Normally Training in Core Teaching skills may be organised at least for eight weeks in one year B.Ed. course. It may be of longer duration in Four Year Integrated Courses.

For practical purpose, we can identify certain Core-Teaching skills as follows:

Some Essential Core Teaching Skills

— Skill of Class Management and Stimulus Variation.
— Skill of Writing Instructional Objectives.
— Skill of Introducing a Lesson (Skill of Introduction).
— Skill of Questioning.
— Skill of Illustrating with Examples.
— Skill of Reinforcement, Feedback and Control.
— Skills for Use of Teaching Aids.
— Skill of Using Blackboard.
— Skill of Closure/Recapitulation/Evaluation.

Format for Skill-Training Sessions

- 5-10 minutes single concept/skill lesson.
- 10-15 students/trainee either of peers or school students. (Student-teachers in simulated situations)
- Focus on a single skill or family of skills in any one skill-training lesson.
- Focused supervision (by supervisor/teacher educator and by peers) which includes both praise and suggestions for improvement.
- Self-evaluation, advanced peer supervision, professional supervision and videotape are all appropriate sources of feedback.
- Reteaching the same lesson is a basic feature of skill training session, ideally after one or two days to reflect on suggestions for improvement. The concept of the reteach session is not remedial. All lessons can be improved with focused supervision and the best lessons taught by the best teachers can be improved the most (Allen, 1994).
- If resources are available a simple one camera video or audio recording of the lesson provides an additional sources of feedback.
- Teacher-educator/supervisors may assist student-teachers in identifying suitable content for specific skill-training.

The training cycle can be presented as follows:

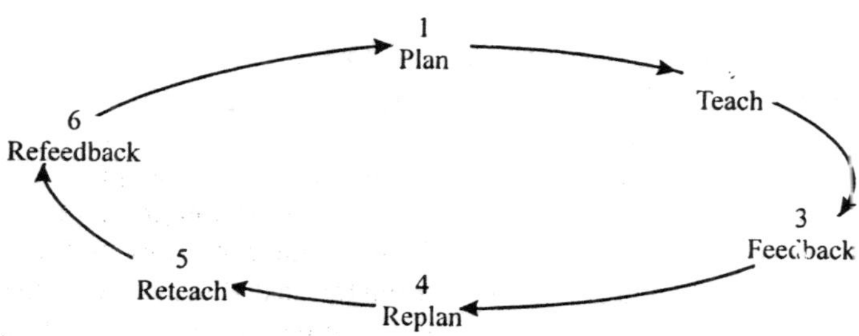

Supervision Protocols for Training in Teaching Skills

Supervision should be focused and balanced between praise and criticism. No more than two suggestions for improvement should be made for any teaching skill lesson, and should be preceded by praise of two of the most important successes in the lesson. Praise and criticism should always go together in the supervision of skill teaching lessons. Praise and criticism should be substantive, not "blowing sunshine" or "blowing thunder," with comments that do not provide instruction on how and what to improve or inform the teacher what specifically has been done well.

Supervision should be balanced between suggestion for the improvement of content and method. Both fundamental aspects of the teaching process must be emphasized in all supervisory protocols.

Supervision is not inspection and evaluation of teaching but the systematic, focused feedback provided for the improvement of instruction.

Supervision and feedback in any fully developed use of teaching skill requires extensive resources. In earlier models of teaching skill supervisory protocols were both detailed and complex, requiring a relatively high level of training for successful supervision. The current recommended approach to skill families and their development envisages a much less precise requirement for supervision. Trial and error learning celebrates approximation in both the practice of the teacher and the suggestions of the supervisor. For this reason it is possible to develop supervisory techniques using self evaluation, peers, advanced peers, and pupils themselves as the source of productive supervision, in addition to professionally trained supervisors.

Use of Teaching Skills in Teacher Training Colleges

Teaching skill can be developed as a course, and it is possible to build on the course concept an expanded use of teaching skills which can be much more systematic and supportive of learner centered education. Even if teaching skill is limited to one or two periods per week, it is possible to divide the class into teaching supervision groups which will allow two students in each group to teach their teaching skill lesson in one class period and to reteach it during the next class period. Depending on group size and the number of periods either one or two teaching skill sessions (teach and reteach) can be taught by each student each term.

An off-time-table teaching skill clinic should be considered as a more comprehensive addition on option. In this format a number of "teaching skill stations" can be established depending on the number of students to be served in the clinic. If the clinic operates for two hours in the late afternoon, 4 days a week, 12 students can be served at each station each week for a complete teaching skill session (teach and reteach). If the teaching skill clinic operates for 8 weeks each term, about 100 students can be served at each station for one session, or 50 students for two sessions each term. The number of stations should allow for a modest extra capacity to provide for absence and scheduling difficulties. Supervision should be the responsibility of all teacher training college teachers and students should be supervised by both education theory and subject teachers over the period of their complete training. Supervision can be developed to include any combination of subject area supervisors, education theory supervisors, advanced peer supervisors and peer supervisors.

An ideal teaching skill clinic would allow each student the opportunity to teach teaching skill sessions for two skills each term for the first year of training, a total of six sessions (teach and reteach) in the case of Two year B.Ed. course. Teaching skill for second year students should be built around opportunities for supervisory experiences and the development of teaching materials. Second year students can be used as supervisors of first year students and their teaching skill course time can be used to train them in supervision skills and get and receive feedback about the results. Groups of second year students can also be assigned the responsibility of making model tapes of instances and non-instances of teaching skills and teaching skill course time can also be used to guide this process.

In the case of Four Year Integrated course it is not recommended that teaching skill be used for third year students. In the third year practice teaching settings, students should be supervised on the actual classroom use of skills learned in teaching as well as other training methods.

Teaching Skills for Schools

Whenever large scale change in instructional methods is desired, it is difficult to encourage and achieve the behaviour changes required of teachers. A school-based teaching skill clinic is an important tool to consider. In this model, groups of teachers work together to learn the new skills by teaching skill demonstration lessons to each other, providing critiques and reteaching the same lessons to see if improvements can be made. In school based teaching skill model video training tapes are very useful to enhance self and peer supervision as external supervision is both difficult to arrange, and is often not well appreciated by a mature teaching staff.

Groups of 4 or 5 teachers are recommended. It will be most effective if teachers are grouped together who have mutual trust and respect. The important focus of school-based teaching skill is that it is used to help good teachers become better, not to remediate weak teachers.

Is school-based clinics it may be desirable to concentrate on one skill for an entire term, urging teachers to try the skill in their classrooms as well as demonstrate it in teaching skill clinic sessions (teach and reteach). A natural outgrowth of the school-based teaching skill clinic is that teachers may become accustomed to critiquing each other in teaching skill sessions and invite each other to observe and critique their actual classes. If this happens, it may be most important outcome of the school-based teaching skill clinic.

Another outcome of the school-based clinic is that school administrators may learn new, supportive supervision roles which can carry over into the classroom, with briefer, more spontaneous classroom observations, and focused supervision.

Teaching Skills in Formal Inservice Teacher Training Programmes

Inservice training programmes will ordinarily use a combination of teaching skill clinic procedures some with formats similar to preservice teacher education clinics (usually during vacation training periods) and school-based teaching skill clinics in association with their continued teaching responsibilities. It is recommended that all inservice teaching skill training focus on skill families.

The Use of Videotape for Teacher Training Skills

The use of videotape feedback has long been a support feature of teaching skill. Early models of teaching skill had to make use of videotapes in a very formal manner, often in specially equipped rooms, the most advanced with two cameras and remote control switching devices. Sound and lighting requirements were very rigorous. As video technology has developed, low light colour cameras with self-contained microphones and self-contained recording units have become much less expensive and have fostered much more casual training procedures for their use. One camera set-ups using basic equipment which is easy to use are recommended with no special room requirements, and multiple teaching skill clinic stations.

Students can be used to operate the cameras. Playback sessions can be held in the evenings with student monitors responsible for the care and proper use of the equipment. Groups of students can be given access to cameorders for the development of model tapes.

Teaching skill does not necessarily require any videotaping at all. The important concept to consider is the value of immediate feedback which can be provided by effective formal supervision. Even the most advanced teaching skill clinics usually have a combination of video and non-video sessions, with each student having access to videotaping sessions at least once during training. Some clinics schedule optional evening sessions, monitored by advanced students where any student or group of students may conduct additional teaching skill sessions with videotaping as desired.

The Development of Model Tapes for Teaching Skills

Model tapes of skills have an important place in teaching skills training. One of the easiest training protocols involves showing positive and negative examples (instances and non-instances) of the skills to be demonstrated in teaching skill. It is strongly recommended that both positive and negative examples of teaching skills be recorded using the same teacher for both. The rationale for using the same teacher for both positive and negative examples is important. Since teaching skill is used as a basic training technique, not for remedial training, we want to be sure to demonstrate the concept that every teacher can be expected to gain the necessary skills with the appropriate training. This underlines the acceptance of trial and error learning as a basic feature of all teacher training. Errors are a normal part of the development of new skills. As teachers learn a new skill it is to be expected that the total quality of the lesson may be reduced as the teacher awkwardly focuses on the new skill being developed.

Model tapes can be made in a variety of ways. Most conventional is for a central training body (curriculum developers for example) to be given the responsibility for making model tapes of the desired skills using teacher training faculty, ministry inspectors or teacher training students as model teachers. Another source of model tapes are videotaped teaching skill sessions where there is a dramatic positive change in the use of the skill from the teach to the reteach session. A third important source of model tapes is to ask advanced teacher training students to make model tapes as a part of their training. Groups of students can be assigned to make one or more model tapes, and given access to videotape facilities when they are not in use.

Model tapes, for example, can be made at the introductory level or with various advanced emphases in each skill family. Model tapes of questioning skills can be made demonstrating asking a required number of questions in a teaching skill lesson (10 in a 5 minute lesson for example), and alternatively teaching the same lesson asking students no questions. A more advanced questioning model tape series can demonstrate positive and negative examples of higher order questions, or another model series could demonstrate the use (and non-use) of probing questions.

Training Support for Teaching Skills

If teaching skill is to be an ongoing training element in both preservice and inservice teacher training programmes, it should have senior staff members responsible to oversee its development and use. Teacher training colleges and schools should be able to call experts for training support in teaching skills. Teacher resource center personnel and support staff should be trained to develop and support teaching skill clinics.

Families of Teaching Skills

These skill families are arbitrary and there is much overlap between the skills. It should be noted that the skill family of lecturing skill is not included because it has been found that this skill is learned in the "background" while other skill families are being trained. The skill family of trial and error learning is also not required to be taught in specific teaching skill sessions but is a pervasive concept to be considered as the basis for all teaching skill instruction.

1. *Questioning Skills*

   — *Number of Questions*
   The introductory questioning skill. Frequency and total number of questions without any judgment of quality. Attention is also given to the spread of questions to all members of the class.

   — *Open-ended Questions*
   Questions which have no specific answer.

   — *Higher Order Questions*
   The skill of asking questions which have no set or defined

answer which encourage thinking and require students to speculate and offer opinions.

— *Probing Questions*
Reaching deeper levels of students awareness, often encouraging students to become aware of new issues and/or positions.

— *The Framing of Questions*
How a question is asked is crucial to its contribution to the learning process. Clarity is a most important requirement.

2. *Reinforcement and Control*

— *Positive and negative reinforcement*
Techniques of reinforcement, positive and negative, with an emphasis on the value of positive reinforcement.

— *Verbal and non-verbal reinforcement*
Both verbal and non-verbal cues from both students and teachers are integral to the teaching learning process.

— *Encouragement*
The skill of encouraging all students, weak and strong. Encouragement stimulates higher levels of performance.

— *Cuing*
The skill to get a positive answer from any student, regardless of how reticent or confused he/she may be.

— *Silence*
Using silence as a tool for control and emphasis. Both positive and negative reinforcement can be given.

— *Selected student focus*
The ability to individualize instruction by selecting one or more students on which to focus attention and provide extra help.

— *Eye contact*
Eye contact compliments a learner, encourages attention, and provides the teacher with valuable information for continuous assessment.

— *Observation*
Becoming more alert to the physical and social environment of the classroom.

— *Conflict resolution*
Alternatives for responding to negavit or unwanted situations in the classroom, and resolving conflicts between students, most often verbal disagreements which become unproductive.

3. *Examples*

— *Relevant examples*
Selecting and using effective examples. All new learning is built on previous knowledge and experience.
— *Analogies and metaphors*
The use of analogies and metaphors to enhance learning.
— *Instances and non-instances*
Building learning from the concrete to the abstract and from the abstract to the concrete. Both are important teaching strategies to learn and use.
— *Concrete-abstract continuum*
Learning can proceed either from the abstract to the concrete or the concrete to the abstract and both strategies are appropriate.

4. *Teaching Aids*

— *Artifacts*
Artifacts are defined as casual objects already available in the environment and require minimal modification for use in the lesson. Effective artefact use makes learning more vivid and memorable.
— *Teaching equipment*
Equipment which is either developed specifically for classroom use or is provided through formal acquisition.
— *Overhead projector*
Effective overhead projector skills
— *Chalkboard*
Effective chalkboard skills making chalkboard use both simple and varied.

5. *Lesson Structure*

— *Lesson introduction*
How to begin a lesson effectively to gain student interest while focusing attention on the objectives of the lesson.
— *Lesson closure*
Effective conclusions to focus concept retention.
— *Assessment*
Continuous assessment must become a habit for all teachers, and is the form of assessment most integral to microteaching.

6. *Cooperative Learning*

— *Paired learning*
This is the form of cooperative learning most appropriate for the microteaching setting. Many principles of cooperative learning can be demonstrated in a paired context.

— *Group learning*
Groups of two or more can be assigned learning tasks independent of teacher presentation.

— *Group monitoring*
The role of the teacher is to facilitate group learning and the monitoring process should encourage trial and error learning.

7. *Learning Principles*

— *Deduction*
Deductive learning does not produce new knowledge, but organizes existing knowledge in more useful ways.

— *Induction*
Based on existing knowledge new knowledge can be incrementally developed.

— *Intuition*
The most important new knowledge is based on intuition and the formation of hypotheses to be tested.

— *Falsification*
Once new knowledge is proposed, the most important method of testing its validity is to try to find counter examples or exceptions. This is an important component of thinking skills.

— *Planned repetition*
Repetition is an important source of learning. Knowledge is "set" through repetition and the exploration of alternative examples.

— *Vividness*
When a concept stands out in a learner's mind, it is remembered easier and longer.

— *Juxtaposition*
Placing ideas, events, or objects in unusual relationships to each other enhances vividness and long term learning.

— *Delayed response*
Learning to wait for 2 or more seconds before responding as a means of encouraging student reflection.

— *Stimulus variation*
Use of a variety of gestures, movement around the classroom, incorporating visual stimuli, and other sensory variation enhances learning.

TRAINING IN ESSENTIAL CORE TEACHING SKILLS

Skills of Class Management and Stimulus Variation

The first and foremost work of the trainee, while entering the class-room is to have a glance on the seating arrangement and sitting position of students. The seats must be properly arranged in rooms, the younger and smaller children along with the visually handicapped and children with hearing impairment be seated in the first and second rows; and elderly/taller students in the back rows. The lesson plan notebook, the supervision diary etc. be placed on the last corner seat convenient to the supervisor.

Skill of class management includes the following skills:

1. Control and modification of facial expression.
2. Greetings and taking up proper positions in the class.
3. Movements (Locomotion) in the class room.
4. Use of appropriate gestures in various situations and various stages.

These need for demonstration of the skill by teacher educators during core-training sessions in simulated situation or actual class room situations.

The following points are to be kept in mind under this skill.

— The practice sessions have to be organised by forming student teachers in groups of ten each under the charge of a teacher-educator.
— For the practice of the skill the content of the activity or the lesson (like mini-lesson, discussion, or practical work etc.) would, however, not be the focus of attention in the practice sessions.
— The appearance of the teacher in the classroom is expected as a cheerful and well composed person.
— Neatness and simplicity is required in the dress and appearance of the student-teacher.

- The practice session has to begin with a demonstration by a teacher-educator in a small group of ten to fifteen student-teachers. This has to be followed at entering the class. Other student-teachers of the group should not upset the teacher entering the class by any remark or mischief. Let him gain the confidence in facing the class. Tell him, without criticism, the appearance he was presenting.
- Observe the student-teacher on his/her

  (a) dress and hair
  (b) confidence
  (c) cheerfulness

The exercise may be repeated

- At the second step observe his/her confidence and facial expression on gesticulation, mimicking and provocation by the group.
- Observe and comment on the facial expression and confidence of the student-teacher.

The practice sessions have to be repeated as long as needed.

- Greeting and taking up proper position in the class

  - Greet the students (by the teacher).
  - Students would also offer greetings on the entry of the teacher (the teacher would respond).
  - Take the central place facing the class.
  - Practice is to be given in simulated situations.

- Movement (Locomotion) in the classroom, neither too much nor stationary.
- Use of Appropriate Gestures in various situations and at various stages (Skill of stimulus variation).
  - Practice on movement in the classroom and expression of gestures of approval, appreciation and disapproval can be had only when some sort of activity is going on.
  - Various forms of activities like reciting poems, discussion on some topic etc. could be used for practice of these skills.

- — For appropriateness of movement depends on balanced supervision and guidance.
- — For practice on gestures patiently understand the views and work done by students before offering reactions.
- — Avoid undue smile or encouragement or displeasure.
- — Give practice in simulated situations and in practice teaching sessions.
- — The teacher can use hand gestures, head and body movements, make certain verbal statement like "Look carefully", "watch what is happening", "Listen carefully" etc.
- — Supplement verbal statement with gesture and body movements to make it more effective.
- — To secure and sustain pupils' attention bring planned variations in your behaviours.
- — The attention drawing behaviours include : (i) Movements, (ii) gestures, (iii) change in speech pattern, (iv) focusing, (v) change in interaction styles, (vi) pausing, (vii) Oral-visual switching.
- — Check what the students are doing (particularly at the back) during movements.

  - — Write on Blackboard.
  - — Do not keep on standing at one place for a long time.
  - — Combine oral messages with gestures by movements of the parts of the body to direct attention, to emphasise importance, to explain emotions, or to indicate shapes, sizes, movements etc.

Observation and Evaluation of Skill of Class Management and Stimulus Variation

The observations can be recorded, during training sessions and practice sessions on the following components of the skill:

(i) Class control and discipline
(ii) Seating arrangement
(iii) Movements (appropriateness and numbers)
(iv) Gestures
(v) Change in speech patterns in tone and speed

(vi) Focusing (verbal, gestural, verbal and gestural).
(vii) Change in interaction styles viz.—
  (a) Teacher Group Interaction.
  (b) Teacher Pupil Interaction.
  (c) Pupil-pupil Interaction.
(viii) Pausing (Silence, asking questions).
(ix) Oral-visual switching
(x) Learning climate of the class.

Skill of Writing Instructional Objectives

The ends of the lesson in view are the instructional objectives. Instructional objectives constitute the desired modification/changes in pupils' behaviour. Such changes may be at thinking level, i.e.; in ideas, thoughts, intellectual operations (Cognitive); feeling level in emotions, attitude, interest, values, sentiments etc. (Affective); and acting level i.e. manipulation, doing by the use of parts of the body, skills (Psychomotor). These changes are interrelated.

The objectives are of two types:

(i) General objectives
(ii) Specific objectives.

The general objectives are broad and subject-based. They cannot be achieved in one lesson. Educational objectives are general objectives viz. "to train pupils in good citizenship", "to develop healthy attitudes among pupils", and the like

The specific objectives are pinpointed, specific behaviours or competency based for a particular lesson. The teacher must be very clear about these behavioural (specific) objectives and plan the activities for the lesson accordingly. Specific objectives are practical and more meaningful to a classroom teacher. They may differ from lesson to lesson. The teacher must identify the specific cognitive, Affective and Psychomotor behaviour modification in students expected on the completion of the lesson.

Specific Cognitive Behavioural objectives can be stated in terms of behavioural modifications related to—

(i) Knowledge (facts, ideas, information, content). What new knowledge is imparted through the lesson.

(ii) Comprehension: Understanding, developing insight into, thinking.
(iii) Application: Abstractions like rules, methods, concepts, general ideas, theories, principles etc.
(iv) Analysis—Ability to analyse various components of the new knowledge.
(v) Synthesis—Ability to synthesis various components.
(vi) Evaluation—Ability to give judgment, finding usefulness and drawbacks.

Similarly Affective Behavioural Objectives may be related to modification in:

(i) Interest (ii) Attitude (iii) Values (iv) Sentiments etc.

Psychomotor Behavioural Objectives can be stated in terms of modification in manipulative skills (i.e. capacity to do something, draw some figure, maps, painting, dancing, swimming, running, riding, jumping, handling, doing, practical works with the help of various parts of the body etc.

Writing Instructional Objectives

Following points should be kept in mind while writing instructional objectives:

— Objectives should be well stated;
— They should be adequate with respect to learning outcome;
— They should be relevant to the content; and
— They should be adequate with respect to the content outline.

The term "well stated" involves communicating clearly, without any ambiguity and misinterpretation what the teacher wants pupils to achieve.

"Adequate with respect to learning outcomes" refers to the coverage of such well-stated objectives in terms of learning outcomes in various domains and levels of learning (Cognitive, Affective and Psychomotor domains and their components in the hierarchy from lower to higher level).

— Objectives must be clearly stated in terms of what specific behavioural change is expected in the learner through the lesson. For example:

1. On the completion of the lesson students will be able:
   — to know . . . .
   — to identity . . . .
   — . . . . to comprehend . . . .
   — . . . . to analyse . . . .
   — . . . . to synthesis . . . .
   — . . . . to evaluate . . . . etc.

2. The following attitudinal change will lake place in students:
   — related to interest
   — related to attitude
   — related to values
   — related to sentiments etc.

3. The students will be able:
   — to draw . . . .
   — to do . . . .
   — to perform . . . .
   — to act . . . .
   — to handle . . . .

— There must be specification of learner performance in observable behavioural terms. The term 'learner performance' implies what the learner is going to do or perform at the end of the instruction i.e. what behavioural change are expected out of the instruction or teaching of that particular lesson.
The term 'Observable behaviour' implies the behaviour (performance, action or operation) that can be observed i.e.; Overt behaviours like naming, classifying, describing etc., Thinking, knowing, understanding, etc. are not observable directly.
   — Use such verbs (in the instructional objectives) that indicate behaviours that are observable directly. For example:

     (i) *knowledge level*—Verbs such as identify, Name label, Read/Decode, select, sort, match, list, define, state etc.
     (ii) *Understanding (Comprehension) analysis, Synthesis,*

Evaluation level—Verbs such as convert, change, paraphrase, Read (Map, Graph etc.), Classify, Categories, Order, Serrate, Differentiate, Discriminate, Compare, Explain, Describe, Summaries Relate, Outline, Interpret, Prove, Justify, Discuss, Give Example, Illustrate, Conclude, Generalise, Infer (message, trend, mood etc.), Predict.

(iii) *Skill level*—Add, substract, solve, compute, Read, Recite, Use in sentence, Analyse-sentence, phrase etc. Numerical Balance equation, list, Compose, Design, Write, Draw Angle, Graph, Map, Colour, Paint, Measure, Set apparatus, support etc.

— Specify condition under which learner performance occurs. Communicate what actually you want the pupils to achieve. Such conditions are nothing but behaviour descriptions.
— Specify the minimum expected level of performance of the learner i.e. how well the learner would be able to perform, minimum level of accuracy to be attained in learner's performance. Some pupils may go beyond the level or standard of performance expected.
— Instructional Objectives should be adequate with respect to learning outcomes.
— Instructional objectives should be relevant to the content.

Setting Behavioural Objectives

Goals and Objectives : Educational goals are broad and abstract. They are important in planning general curricular objectives. Behavioural objectives are precise and measurable. They are designed for individual classrooms or even individual students. Because behavioural objectives are specific, they are much narrower than educational goals.

— A behavioural objective is what a student or a class will be expected to do in an observable way after the teacher has taught.
— Objectives are translation of purposes into the specific performances that represent the terminal behaviours of students in a unit or a course.
— Goals are broadly philosophical, global, nonmeasurable, almost timeless in their application and directional in their intent.

— Behavioural objectives manifest themselves in learners activities that are operational measurable, relatively time bound, highly specific and discretly quantifiable.

(a) The Cognitive Domain Taxonomy

1. *Knowledge*
   — Knowledge of specifics
   — Knowledge of ways and means of dealing with specifics
   — Knowledge of universals and abstractions in a field.
2. *Comprehension*
   — Translation
   — Interpretation
   — Extrapolation
3. *Application*
4. *Analysis*
   — Analysis of elements
   — Analysis of relationships
   — Analysis of organisational principles.
5. *Synthesis*
   — Production of a unique communication
   — Production of a plan, or proposed set of operation
   — Derivation of a set of abstract relations.
6. *Evaluation*
   — Judgment in terms of internal evidence
   — Judgement in terms of external criteria.

(b) The Affective Domain Taxonomy

1. *Receiving (Attenting)*
   — Awareness
   — Willingness to receive
   — Controlling or selected attention
2. *Responding*
   — Acquiescence in responding
   — Willingness to respond
   — Satisfaction in response
3. *Valuing*
   — Acceptance of a value, preference for a value
   — Commitment

4. *Organization*
   — Conceptualization of a value
   — Organization of a value system
5. *Characterisation by a value complex*
   — Generalized set
   — Characterization

(c) The Psychomotor Domain Taxonomy

1. *Reflex movements*
   — Sequential reflexes
   — Inter sequential reflexes
   — Supra sequential reflexes
2. *Basic Fundamental Movements*
   — Locomotor movements
   — Non-locomotor movements
   — Manipulative movements
3. *Perceptual Abilities*
   — Kinesthetic discrimination
   — Visual discrimination
   — Auditory discrimination
   — Tactile discrimination
   — Coordinated abilities
4. *Physical Abilities*
   — Endurance
   — Strength
   — Flexibility
   — Agibility
5. *Skilled Movements*
   — Simple adaptive skills
   — Compound adaptive skills
   — Complex adaptive skills
6. *Non-discursive communication*
   — Expressive movements
   — Interpretive movements.

Observation and Evaluation of Skill of Writing Instructional Objectives

Skill of Writing Instructional objectives can be evaluated on the following points:

(i) Learner specified
(ii) Performance in observable behaviour
(iii) Conditions specified
(iv) Minimum level of performance specified
(v) Cognitive domain: Higher level and lower level
(vi) Affective domain
(vii) Psychomotor domain
(viii) Relevant to the content

SKILL OF INTRODUCING A LESSON (SKILL OF INTRODUCTION)

For introducing the lessons the teacher has to make use of the previous knowledge/entering behaviour of pupils in that content area. To make the new knowledge (lesson) a unified and interwoven part of his "Apperceptive mass" the teacher must evoke the previous experience of the pupils in that area so that the new knowledge may be properly linked with the existing knowledge of pupils. It is a process quite similar to the threading of beads in a garland. That is why in lesson planning previous knowledge follows introduction step. Introductory questions should be based on the previous knowledge related to the present content and then the teacher has to proceed from 'Known to Unknown'.

While introducing the lesson the teacher has to create such conditions through questioning audio-visual aids, Short stories or narrating such instance which provide sufficient clue for the present lesson. It arouses curiosity of students and makes them attentive to the present lesson apart from motivating them and arousing their interest.

Thus if any new knowledge is to be added to the previous knowledge of the learner there should be a logical continuity between them. The new knowledge should get integrated, assimilated and accommodated with the previous knowledge or entering behaviours to get the apperceptive mass of the learner enriches.

Therefore, the teachers should be aware of the previous knowledge of students of a particular age and grade level.

— For introducing a lesson the teachers can make use of devices like

(a) Use of examples, analogies, similarities.
(b) Questioning (introductory questions based on the previous knowledge of students related to the present lesson).

(c) Lecturing, describing, narrating, illustrating.
(d) Story telling, describing related instance.
(e) Role playing, dramatization.
(f) Use of audio-visual aids
(g) Experimentation, demonstration etc.

— Use of device should be suitable to the maturity level, age level, grade level, interest, culture, experience of pupils and also to the unit or lesson to be taught.
— More than one device can be used for desirable effect.
— There must be continuity or sequence of ideas or information being presented. The teacher's statement or questions should be relate to the immediately preceding question or statement.
— The teacher's statement or question must relate to the present lesson and its aim.

Observation and Evaluation of Skill of Introducing a Lesson

The skill of introducing a lesson can be observed and evaluated on the following points:

(i) Use of the previous knowledge of students.
(ii) Continuity or sequencing of questions and statements.
(iii) Relevance of questions and statements to the present topic or lesson.
(iv) Appropriateness of device used in terms of age, grade, and maturity level of students.

Skill of Questioning

Questioning is very significant technique in teaching. Actually the development of lesson and the assimilation of the new knowledge with the previous one depends on how and which questions are put to evoke the knowledge and curiosity of the students for the new knowledge.

There may be various types of questions like Introductory Questions, Thought Provoking Questions, Prompting Questions, Probing Questions, Information Seeking Questions, Refocusing Questions, Redirected Questions, Increasing Critical Awareness Questions, Open-ended Questions, Higher Order Question, 'Yes' 'No' Type Questions, and Recapitulatory Questions etc.

The effectiveness of questions depends on their appropriate use. During teacher training and teaching sufficient practice is required for framing questions and their use at various stages or steps of teaching.

Purpose of Questions

(i) To Stimulate analytical thought.
(ii) Diagnose student difficulties.
(iii) Determine progress towards specific goals.
(iv) Motivate students.
(v) Clarify and expand concepts.
(vi) Encourage new appreciations and attitudes.
(vii) Give specific directions to thinking
(viii) Relate cause to effect
(ix) Encourage student self-evaluation
(x) Encourage the application of concepts.

At the introduction step Introductory Questions based on the previous knowledge of the students are put before the class to evoke the entering behaviour of the students or to bring to the consciousness the knowledge and experience related to present lesson. The teacher must have insight into the mental state of the students. The questions should be interesting and evoking curiousity but simple and understandable by students. By putting sequential questions leading to desired goal of guessing the topic by the students the teacher on the one hands makes the students aware of or conscious of their existing knowledge about the present day lesson and on the other hand makes them attentive and curious for the declaration of the topic by the teacher. Thus the purpose of Introductory Questions is solved and by now the students have been sufficiently motivated for the present lesson.

— During the presentation of the lesson Developing Questions, Thought Provoking Questions and Probing Questions are to be used. The purpose of putting such questions is to develop the lesson with the help of students. "Teaching is not telling, it is training to learn". This training in solving problem, in thinking, in reflection and originality is provided by creating such psychological environment in the class by putting questions and using various teaching learning aids where students themselves discover knowledge or create the desire knowledge.

— At the Recapitulation step Recapitulatory Questions are put to test whether the students have properly grasped the lesson or not Recitulotary Questions are based on the main messages of the lesson and its generalisation. Therefore, they are general in nature and evaluate students learning upto this stage. If these questions are not properly answered by students, it indicates that reteaching, classification and explanation is required. The teacher can do that.

The following points are significant for training in skill of questioning:

1. *Training in skill of questioning:*
   — The questions should be well structed i.e.
   — The language of questions must be grammatically correct for proper understanding of its meaning.
   — The questions should be concise in words, direct and straight forward without any ambiguity.
   * The questions should be relevant i.e. related to the topic— and related to the previous experience of the student.
   * The questions should be specific or pin-pointed.

2. *Under "Process" of questioning due care should be taken that:*

   (i) The speed of questioning should be appropriate. The teacher should speak out questions neither too hurriedly nor too slowly for proper comprehension and attention. The teacher should give sufficient pause after the question in order to enable the pupils to understand the question.
   (ii) The voice of the teacher should be audible and clear to all the students in the class. It should be in a raised voice; but in a pleasant tone and in a friendly manner.
   — Unnecessary repetition of questions by the teacher should be avoided.
   — Answers given by students should not be repeated by the teacher.
   — 'Yes' or 'No' type questions should be avoided. These questions encourage guess work among the pupils and do not stimulate them to think deeply.
   — Elliptical questions are also not good questions. Questions which require completion to get the answer are elliptical questions. For example:

(a) Your name is . . . .?
(b) A noun is a . . . .?
(c) Mount Everest was conquered by . . . .?

Such questions should be avoided. Suggestive questions should also be avoided where the questions are asked just after the concept or fact has been taught. These questions are also called 'echo' questions. For example:

Teacher—India is a big country. It has many state. Delhi is the capital of India.

Q—Tell me, what is Delhi?
Pupil—Delhi is the capital of India.

In such questions, there is no thinking on the part of the learners. They just reproduce the told facts. Therefore such questions should not be asked.

— Rhetorical questions which are followed by the statement of the teacher without the reply given by the students should also be avoided. For example:

Teacher—Isn't it a horrible scene in the picture? Surely, even elders will be afraid to look at it . . . .

Specific Suggestions

Specific helps can be drawn from the psychological principles most frequently involved in the use of questions. These suggestions, however, are not intended to serve as a substitute for an understanding of the basic principles, but they should serve as pointed reminders of certain things to remember and certain things to avoid.

Recommendations

1. Use specific kinds of questions to serve specific purpose.
2. Use thought-provoking questions frequently.
3. Use quick, random questions for review.
4. Use related questions that become progressively more difficult if you want students to acquire concepts in depth.
5. Ask questions only when you have a definite purpose for doing so.

6. Ask questions that are within the pupils own range of experience and knowledge.
7. Ask questions that are free of confusing parenthetical elements.
8. Word questions as simply as possible without distorting meaning.
9. If you wish to have a question answered in a certain way (compare, classify, outline, define, etc.). Indicate this clearly.
10. Only accept student replies that are reasonably complete and meaningful.
11. If students do not answer your questions with reasonable completeness and accuracy, make sure the class is not left with false concepts.
12. As a general rule, use some portion of a student's answer if only to encourage him and keep him interested.
13. Establish a classroom climate in which students will feel free to ask questions.
14. Before asking for a response to a thought question, allow students time to think about it.

Cautions

1. As a general rule, don't ask obvious questions.
2. Don't react emotionally if the student fails to answer a question correctly.
3. Don't ask "Are there any questions?" as a device for determining whether students have understood the lesson. Usually you will get no response even when students do not understand.
4. Don't allow the questioning procedure to lead you and your students away from the planned subject.
5. Don't ask ambiguous questions.
6. Don't direct your questions to a few isolated students. Include as many students are possible in your questioning.
7. Don't attempt to bluff if you are not sure of the answer to a student's question. Say "I don't know" and then find out.
8. Don't discourage student responses to student questions.
9. Don't ask catch questions.
10. Don't ask question that call for two different and confusing reactions to the same question.
11. Don't ask questions that contain words not understood by students.

12. As a general rule don't repeat questions. Insist that students listen to what you say.

Probing Questions

If students do not give fully correct response but partially correct one or, sometimes, they do not respond at all then the teacher has to probe or to prompt or to give some clue or hint for correct answer by asking a number of questions about what they already know. Thus the teacher leads them to the correct response to remove the difficulty or hindrance in their understanding.

— The teacher has to deal with different types of responses such as no response, incomplete response, partially correct response and completely correct response. He may give certain hints or clue to the pupil who may give the correct response. Thus he may use prompting technique to help the pupil to give correct response

  — Thus the pupils get encourage and develop confidence that they can give correct response.

— The teacher can seek further information about pupil response by prompting.
— By refocusing the pupil response the teacher helps the pupil to view the correct response from a different view point and to develop deep thinking.
— The teacher may redirect the same questions to many pupils to respond when there is no response, incomplete, partially correct or wrong response.
— The teacher may put questions such as 'how' and 'why' of the correct response. Such questions increase the critical awareness of the pupils about the response.

The sum up, the components of the skill of probing questions are:

(i) Prompting technique
(ii) Seeking further information technique
(iii) Refocusing technique
(iv) Redirection technique, and
(v) Increasing critical awareness technique.

The purposes of using such techniques are:

(i) to lead the pupil from a 'no' or 'wrong' response to the criterion or desired response by step-by-step questioning process;
(ii) to clarify pupil's understanding about the response;
(iii) to help the pupil to view the response from a broader perspective.
(iv) to involve more and more pupils in the discussion; and
(v) to increase critical awareness in the pupils.

Observation and Evaluation of Skill of Questioning

The skill of Questioning can be observed and evaluated on the following points:

(i) Questions were grammatically correct.
(ii) Questions were relevant to the topic discussed.
(iii) Questions were specific and concise.
(iv) Questions were put with proper speed and pause.
(v) Questions were put to the class with proper voice.
(vi) Questions were not repeated unnecessarily.
(vii) Responses to the questions were not repeated.
(viii) The teachers used prompting questions to lead the pupils to the expected response.
(ix) The teacher used questions for seeking further information of the pupils responses.
(x) The teacher used questions to refocus the pupil responses.
(xi) The teacher redirected questions to the pupils.
(xii) The teacher used questioning to increase critical awareness of the pupils about their responses.

Skills of Explaining and Illustrating with Examples

During the course of teaching learning process, at times, situations arise, where a simple narration or description of a phenomenon, event or principle does not bring desirable understanding on the part of the learner. To explain properly, the cause and effect of a phenomenon or how and why of an event it becomes necessary to put the ideas in a systematic way. They should be logically arranged also.

A teacher is said to be explaining when he is describing 'how', 'why' or sometimes 'what' of a concept, event principle, condition or phenomenon. Thus explaining can be defined as an activity to bring about an understanding in someone about a concept, principle etc. An explanation is generally around a phenomenon, action and various steps involved in arriving at a particular result. Reasons for the conditions are given.

There are various techniques through which we can explain an idea, phenomenon etc. We can use examples, or even perform an experiment or demonstration. We can use audio-visual aids. Sometimes, we can use all these techniques simultaneously. For effective teaching, the teacher should practise more and more of desirable behaviour like using explaining links, using beginning and concluding statements and testing pupils' understanding by putting a few questions and avoiding the use of undesirable behaviours like making irrelevant statements, lacking in continuity, using inappropriate vocabulary, lacking in fluency, and using of vague words and phrase as far as possible. A glossary of the key, terms is given below:

(i) *Explaining links* : words and phrases (mostly conjunctions and prepositions) that should be used during explaining.

the result of	in order of	the function of
therefore	in order than	the purpose of
hence	since	the implication
as a result	because	of next
consequently	so that	before
that's why due	what . . . if	through
to this is now	why but	thus

(ii) *Beginning statement(s)* : Introductory statement made upto the point where explanation begins.

(iii) *Concluding statement(s)* : Summary statements covering the main results in the explanation which are stated after the explanation ends.

(iv) *Irrelevant statement(s)* : Statements not related to what is being explained and does not contribute to its understanding.

(v) *Lacking in continuity* : Refers to break in the ideas of information being presented during explaining. The following are such situations:

1. When a statement is not logically related to the previous statement.
2. When a topic already taught is referred to without showing any relationship to what is being explained;
3. When there is no sequence of space or place;
4. When there is no sequence of time; and
5. When the statements are irrelevant.

(vi) *Inappropriate Vocabulary* : All the technical terms used are inappropriate to the particular class or age group and unknown to most of the pupils (unless teacher stops and explained).

(vii) *Lacking in fluency* : All half sentences and sentence reformulated in the middle.

(viii) *Vague words and phrases* : Words and phrases which indicate that teacher is failing to make something explict. (Some of them are given below):

some	much	seems
many	something	somewhat
things	probably	the rest
a little	perhaps	almost
might	may	types of
few	in fact	actually

Includes words and phrases such as 'you see' ('okey', 'correct' etc. which form a part of teacher mannerisms.

An explanation will generally be around a phenomenon, action, result, condition, or an event. While giving explanation about any one of them the teacher will be giving causes for the phenomenon, reasons behind the action, various steps involved in arriving at the particular result, reasons for the condition or various events that have occurred earlier resulting in the event being explained. All such causes, reasons, steps, events etc. are called antecedents. Such antecedents result in the phenomenon, event, conditions, result or action. Each one of them (phenomenon, event, condition, result, or action) is known as a consequent. Thus, an explanation involves giving antecedents to a consequent which can be diagrammatically represented as follows:

Antecedents	Explanation	Consequent
(Causes, reasons, action, steps, events	⟶	(Phenomenon, action, result, event, condition)

Sometimes, while explaining, the teacher will be giving the consequents or consequences of a phenomenon, action, event or result being explained. This is diagrammatically shown below:

Antecedents (Phenomenon, action, result, event, condition)	Explanation ←	Consequent (Phenomenon, action, result, event, condition)

— Every statement made by the teacher should be relevant to the phenomenon being explained. There should be continuous flow of ideas. That is to say every statement should be logically linked with the preceding statement and forthcoming statement.

— Such words or statements which are not known to students should not be used by the teachers. In other words the teacher should use vocabulary known to pupils.

— The teacher should be fluent in speech and no half sentence should be uttered.

— The desirable teacher behaviours to be practised in order to develop the skill of explaining are:

(i) Using explaining links i.e.; since, after, as a result, therefore, in order to etc.
(ii) Using beginning and concluding statements.
(iii) Testing pupils understanding.

— Undesirable teacher behaviours as given below are to be avoided:

(i) Stating irrelevant statements.
(ii) Lacking in continuity in statements.
(iii) Using in appropriate vocabulary.
(iv) Lacking in fluency.
(v) Using vague words or sentences.

Illustrating with Examples

The skill of illustrating with examples helps in bringing clarity, simplicity and interest in teaching. This skill is effective as it takes the learners from knows to unknown. It also secures and sustains the attention of pupils and hence creates interest in the lesson. It makes difficult ideas easy.

— In order to convey abstract ideas, concepts and laws the teacher should try to give a shape to these in such a way that interest and curiosity are aroused and the concept is also clarified.

— Difficult ideas, concepts and theories can be conveyed better by giving concrete examples from the experience of pupils. They attempt to realise unfamiliar through familiar. Therefore, the teacher should lead the pupils from simple to complex concepts.

— Examples are situations or objects in which principles, ideas, or concepts are being applied. The skill of illustrating with examples involves describing an idea, concept, or principle by using various types of examples.
The teacher has:

(i) to formulate suitable examples related to an idea, concept, or law;
(ii) to present the examples in the most effective manner to the pupils; and
(iii) to verify by asking examples from the pupils whether learners have understood or not.

— The examples should have the following characteristics:

(i) they should be simple,
(ii) they should be relevant to the concept or rule they illustrate, and
(iii) they should be interesting to the pupils.

— Examples can be visual, auditory and tactual (related to the sense of touch).

(i) Visual examples involve presentation of objects, models, pictures, graph etc.
(ii) Oral examples are auditory in nature.
(iii) Tactual examples involve use and manipulation of objects, doing by hand or any part of the body etc.

— Examples can be verbal and non-verbal

(i) Verbal examples include giving analogies, story telling etc.
(ii) Non-verbal media include objects, models, pictures, diagrams, maps, sketches and experimentaldemonstrations.

— There are two basic approaches which a teacher can make use of while teaching. They are:

(i) Inductive Approach
(ii) Deductive Approach

— In Inductive approach the teacher starts with examples relevant to the concept or rule and makes an inference or generalisation or conclusion on the basis of particular examples

P (Particulars) ⟶ G (General)

— In Deductive Approach the teacher states the ideas, principle, concept or rule first and then he gives examples which illustrate, clarify, substantiate the idea or prove the rule or principle.

G (General) ⟶ P (Particulars)

— Inducto-Deductive Approach involves following inductive approach in the beginning while clarifying or arriving at a concept or rule. This is followed by the stating of the concept or rule with the help of pupils from the examples. Then the teacher has to verify the understanding of pupils (deduction) by asking them to give examples related to the concept or rule.

The teacher initiates and elicits related examples from pupils' experience to clarify the concept or rule	→	Stating of Concept or rule with the help of examples	→	Teacher elicits examples from Pupils to verify their understanding pupils give examples

Examples ⟶ Rule ⟶ Example

— Thus, following are the important components of the skill of Illustrating with examples:

(i) Formulating simple examples,
(ii) Formulating examples relevant to the idea or the rule,
(iii) Formulating interesting examples,
(iv) Using appropriate media for examples, and
(v) Using examples by inducto-deductive approach.

Observation and Evaluation of Skills of Explaining and Illustrating with Examples

They can be observed on the following points:

(i) Used

(a) explaining links
(b) beginning statements
(c) concluding statements

(ii) Put sufficient questions to test pupils' understanding and correct responses
(iii) Used irrelevant statements
(iv) Lacked continuity in explaining
(v) Used in appropriate vocabulary
(vi) Lacked fluency in explaining
(vii) Used vague words and phrases
(viii) Examples were simple interesting relevant to the concept or rule
(ix) The media used for examples were appropriate
(x) Pupils gave relevant examples
(xi) The examples were sufficient
(xii) Pupils have clearly understood the concept or rule

Skill of Reinforcement, Feedback and Control

Reinforcement is one of the most widely known principles of successful learning. Any environmental event that is programmed as a consequence of a response that can increase the rate of responding is called reinforcer. Reinforcement is psychological in nature. It is condition or situation which increases the probability of desirable responses and also decreases the probability of undesirable responses.

The term feedback is a functional one for description. It is an inherent part of internal control in communication. The output from a system which is returned as input to control future output is called feedback. This feedback is used by the learner to modify his subseqent responses. There are two main functions of feedback-regulation and control. The control function leads to the desirable direction. The regulation modifies the situation or behaviour. The term 'encouragement' denotes, here, the skill of encouraging all students, weak and strong. Encouragement stimulates higher levels of performance.

— Rewarded responses tend to be repeated in given situations, unrewarded responses tend to be discontinued. This 'Law of Effect' is at the root of reinforcement. There may be 'Positive Reinforcement' and 'Negative Reinforcement'. Positive Reinforcement means strengthening of desirable behaviour by praise, smile encouraging words and nonverbal cues. Positive reinforcers increase pupils' participation in the class. Negative Reinforcement means weakening of undesirable behaviours of pupil by discouraging expressions or words by the teacher. Negative Reinforcers decrease pupils' participation in the class.

— The teacher should use more Positive Reinforcers which are those behaviours of the teacher which encourage the pupils to participate more and more in learning activities. He should generate pleasing effect on the pupil for their desirable behaviours.

— He should use less Negative Reinforcers which are those behaviours of the teacher which discourage the students to participate. Negative Reinforcers have punishing effect (unpleasant) on the pupils.

> Skill of Reinforcement involves the use of the positive reinforcers more and more and decreases the use of negative reinforcers so that the pupils participate to the maximum.

— The teacher may give Positive Verbal Reinforcement through various verbal (with words) expressions. He has to accept the feelings and the ideas of the pupils.

— Pupils' suggestions may be paraphrased by restating the idea more clearly. The teacher can make encouraging remarks such as 'that's good', 'right', 'yes', 'correct', 'fine', 'excellent', "splendid', 'well done', 'go-ahead', 'carry on' etc. Extra verbal expressions such as 'hm-hm', 'uh-uh' will also reinfoce pupils' behaviour.

— The teacher can use certain Positive Non-verbal Reinforcement (without words) with expressions like nodding of head, smiling, moving towards the responding pupil, keeping eyes on the pupil, giving ears to the pupil indicating that attention is being paid to the pupil's words, writing the response of the pupil on the blackboard, or any other non-verbal action indicating pleasure at the pupil's response.

— The teacher should avoid Negative Verbal Reinforcement. He should avoid discouraging statements such as 'I do not like what you are doing', 'do something else', 'nonsense', 'you are not good', 'no', 'wrong', 'incorrect', 'stop it', 'that's not', etc., or discouraging cues and voice tones as 'humph' in sarcastic voice. These affect learning negatively and decrease the motivation of the pupils.

— Similarly Negative Non-verbal Reinforcement such as behaviours as frowning, moving away from the responding pupil, discouraging looks, hard and disapproving stares, not looking at the responding pupil, tapping foot impatiently etc. should also be avoided.

— The teacher should try to involve all the pupils and encourage their participation. Encouraging or reinforcing only a few responding pupils results in the neglect of the passive pupils and shy pupils.

— Wide range of reinforcing statements should be used and not only the same one of two statements every time.

— At the same time over use of reinforcement should be avoided.

Observation and Evaluation of Skills of Reinforcement, Feedback and Control

This skill can be observed and evaluated on the following points:

(i) Use of positive verbal reinforcers

(ii) Use of extra-verbal cues
(iii) Use of positive non-verbal cues
(iv) Use of negative verbal and non-verbal reinforcement
(v) Wrong/inappropriate use of Reinforcement
(vi) Providing encouragement
(vii) Use of silence for control and emphasis
(viii) Reinforcing selected students
(ix) Conflict resolution
(x) No reinforcement even when required

Skills for Use of Teaching Aids

Practice on skills under this head does not require formation of groups of student-teachers. Each student-teacher may, therefore be given practice sessions where they can work independent of others. In the evaluation of performances and for feedback purposes, the final product as well as the process has to be looked at by at least one student-teacher. For general practice, therefore, each student-teacher may work individually but for providing feedback on performances, groups of two or three student-teachers may be formed.

Selection of Teacher Aids

This implies looking at two major considerations. The first is the needs of the lesson and the second is the availability of teaching aids in a given situation. The first exercise, therefore, has to be to acquaint the student-teachers with teaching aids available in schools and colleges. Visits to local schools can be profitably arrange for this purpose. In the second exercise after this general acquaintance with available materials, the student-teachers may be asked to select a lesson from the textbooks used in schools and to identify the teaching aids needed for effective teaching of the lesson. The group can discuss the appropriateness of the teaching aids suggested by a teacher for a particular lesson.

Preparation of Charts, Models, Maps and Diagrams

Demonstration by teacher-educators (or specialists) with reference to the preparation of each of these items is necessary. The boldness of sketches, the spacing, the colour combinations and the educative value of the materials produced are to be the focal points for feedback and evaluation. Each student-teacher may be required to prepare at least one item of each type with reference to a particular lesson. The linking up to the teaching aid with a lesson has to be emphasised for proper feedback and evaluation.

Operation of Mechanical Aids

The exercise in this context has to be that of handling the teaching aids available in the training institute. Gadgets like tape recorders, magic lanterns, slide projectors, record players, etc., cannot be used by the teachers, unless they have enough experience of handling them. Two aspects of work are involved in it. The first is, as mentioned above, a mechanical handling of the gadget as a mechanic. This can be practised by all the student-teachers both individually as well as in groups according to available facilities. The other aspect, which is more important, is the use of these aids in the classroom. The positioning of the teacher, the commentary on slides, the speed of operation, etc., are all important considerations in taking advantage of these aids. It would, therefore, be desirable to arrange practice seasons, where each student-teacher by turn, would teach mini-lessons with the help of these aids.

Observation and Evaluation of Skills for Use of Teaching Aids

On following points:

1. Appropriateness of teaching aids.
2. Proper handling.
3. Relevant use.
4. Suitability of teaching aids to the class.
5. Size, lettering and attractiveness.

Skill of Using Blackboard

Blackboard or chalkboard is the visual aid most widely used by the teacher for classroom instruction. Each student-teacher requires enough practice to learn the art of writing on the blackboard.

The skill of using blackboard consists of following components:

1. Legibility of handwriting.
2. Neatness in the blackboard work.
3. Appropriateness of written work on the blackboard.

The importance of skillful use of the blackboard can be stated as follows:

(i) A good blackboard work brings about clarity of concepts through clear visual presentation.
(ii) It reinforces the matter presented verbally.
(iii) If used properly blackboard work gives holistic picture of the lesson.
(iv) It adds variety to the lesson and draws attention of the pupils.

Following points should be kept in mind while writing on the blackboard.

— Writing on blackboard should be bold enough so that students from the back bench in the class can easily read.
— The teacher must check whether there is glare on the blackboard.
— A good blackboard work should give holistic picture of the lesson taught i.e. students, at the end of the lesson can easily recollect what has been taught.
— Important points should be underlined which may draw students' attention.
— A good blackboard work may contain the important points in the lesson. The details are not necessary.
— The teacher's handwriting should be legible. Legibility is one of the important component of a good blackboard work for ease in reading it. Legibility includes following points:

(a) Every letter should be distinct.
(b) There should be adequate spacing between two letters and two words.
(c) The slantness of each letter should be closest to the vertical.
(d) The size of the letters should be large enough to be read from the far end of the room.
(e) Capital and small letters should be of appropriate size.
(f) The thickness of the lines should be the same.

— There should be Neatness in blackboard work as follows:

(a) The words and sentences should be written in the horizontal lines parallel to the base of the blackboard.

(b) There should be adequate spacing between the lines.
(c) There should be no over writing.
(d) Relevant matter should be retained on the blackboard for further discussion.

— There should be Appropriateness of work on the blackboard which includes continuity, brevity and simplicity, drawing attention and focusing.
— The blackboard summary should be brief and simple.
— Underline those points to which attention of pupils is to be drawn.
— Use coloured chalks sparingly to bring about contrast with other matter presented on the blackboard.
— Illustrations and diagrams should be simple, large and clear enough to convey the ideas presented.
— Avoid unnecessary details.
— Check the condition (smoothness) for usability of the blackboard.
— The light falling on the blackboard should neither be too bright nor too dim to protect the eyes of pupils from strain.
— Check whether or not the blackboard is clean enough before and after use.
— Stand on one side of the blackboard and do not come in between the pupils and the blackboard.
— Use a pointer for explaining various points.
— Never use finger for erasing.
— Avoid committing mistakes in the content written on the blackboard.

Observation and Evaluation of the Skill of Using Blackboard

It can be evaluated on the following points:

(i) Legibility of handwriting—
(Distinct letters, spacing, slantness, size of the letter, capital and small letters, thickness of lines)
(ii) Neatness in the blackboard work—
(Letters and words in straight line and parallel to the base of blackboard, spacing between lines, overwriting, relevant matter retained)

(iii) Appropriateness of written work—
(Continuity in the points, brief and simple points, important points underlined, suitable use of coloured chalks, diagrams and illustrations)

(iv) Miscellaneous points—
(Glare of blackboard, cleanliness, position of teacher, mistakes in writing)

Skill of Closure/Recapitulation

To know that objectives have been achieved, pupils have learnt what they intended to learn, what have been taught was appropriate to the objectives of the lesson and to know how can pupils fuse new learning with the previous learning the teacher must be skilled in the skill of closure or recapitulation or evaluation.

'Recapitulation' or 'Closure' is a process of associating new facts with the old knowledge, applying new knowledge in various situations and repetition of the facts in the best possible way. It is generally necessary to use this skill for definite summing up and revision of the lesson. It is a type of generalisation or review of the facts taught. The main points covered during the lesson are synthesised into a meaningful whole.

The components of the skill of closure or recapitulation are:

(i) Consolidation of the major points,
(ii) Providing opportunity for the pupils to apply new knowledge to new situations, and
(iii) Linking the pupils new knowledge with their previous knowledge as well as with future knowledge.

The following steps can be taken for this skill:

— The teacher can consolidate the main points by putting a few questions based on the lesson taught.
— Only a few questions should be asked and each question should be logically linked with the teacher's previous questions and the pupil's preceding response.
— Consolidation of the main points can be done by making certain statements and side by side developing a diagram on the blackboard using summary statements and developing blackboard

summary by the teacher.

— Other non-verbal media like models, charts, etc. can also be used for consolidation.

— In providing opportunities for pupils to apply present knowledge in various situations the teacher may again use questioning—oral or/and written, non-verbal media like diagrams, maps charts etc. or/and experimentation. This involves creating situations where the pupils can make use of what they have learnt during the lesson (present knowledge) in solving the problems in new situations or different situations.

— Linking past knowledge with the present knowledge involves helping the pupils to see the relationship between them. Any new learning should be meaningfully fused with the apperceptive mass of the pupils. It can be done by pointing to the contrasts or bringing similarity between the both new and previous knowledge. The teacher can make pupils review their past knowledge. He can follow questioning, summary statements, using non-verbal media like blackboard, maps, charts etc. and experimentation for this purpose.

— Linking present knowledge with future learning includes appropriate home work or assignments given to the pupils. The appropriate assignments should:

(i) suit the maturity level of the pupils.
(ii) provide the opportunities for the pupils to apply the present knowledge in new situations,
(iii) demand the application of higher mental processes rather than the mere recalling of the present knowledge.

Assignments may be given in different forms, such as:

(i) in the form of broad questions or objective type questions.
(ii) problems for pupils to find solutions or do experiments.
(iii) Preparation of charts, diagrams, etc.

Observation and Evaluation of Skill of Closure/Recapitulation

Skill of closure on recapitulation or evaluation can be observed on the following points:

(i) Consolidation of major points with/without pupils'

involvement;

(ii) Opportunities provided to pupils to apply new knowledge;

(iii) Linking of present knowledge with the previous knowledge (Comparison and contrast);

(iv) Home work and assignments.

Core-Training : Resume

Core-Training aims at enabling the student-teachers to acquire mastery of manipulative skills needed by the teachers to be effective in their teaching work.

Practise and Develop Mastery of Skills Pertaining to the Following Areas

1. *Skills of Class Management*:
   (i) Control and modification of facial expressions
   — Cheerful appearance, composed person.
   — Not shy, nervous or perlexed.
   — Confidence, a balanced person.
   — Neatness and simplicity in dress and appearance.
   (ii) Greeting and taking up proper position in the class:
   — To greet the students.
   — To take central place facing the classroom.
   (iii) Movements (locomotion) in the classroom.
   (iv) Use of appropriate gestures in various situations and at various stages:
   — Balanced supervision of the class.
   — Watchful eye on all the students.
   — Listen students patiently and understand them.
   — No undue smile or encouragement.

2. *Skills of Communication (Teacher Acts)*

   Attention may be paid to the following:
   (a) Pauses
   (b) Modulation of voice
   (c) Pitch and volume of voice.
   (d) Facial expression
   (i) Narration
   — Art of articulated speech making

— Feedback may be provided by video tape recorder if possible
— Recorded narrations may also be used for model demonstration
— Scripts and notes be prepared by student-teachers.

(ii) Recitation

— Rhythmic rendering of verses without music
— Facial expression, modulation, pitch of voice
— Enough practice and feedback
— Selection of poems and songs from the textbook

(iii) Dramatisation

— Visual nad audio environment
— Mono acting
— Short events
— Appropriate facial expression
— Modulation of voice, movements, pauses
— Creation of appropriate environments
— Proper sequence of presentation
— Guided points for feedback and evaluation.

(iv) Explanation

— Paraphrasing and elaboration
— Substantiating the main points with anecdotes and facts
— Relevant and adequate supplementary material.

(v) Demonstration

— Selection of right type of activity or apparatus
— Use of small steps
— Explanation on each step
— Laying stress on the main step of demonstration
— Feedback and evaluation based on the right type of activity.

3. *Skills or Interaction (Teacher-Pupil Acts)*

— Interaction between teacher and students
— Pre-planning and spontaneous decision making
— Stimulus by the teacher and students
— Adequate practice sessions

I. Questioning and Feedback

(a) Framing various types of questions
— Formulating questions spontaneously requires practice

- — Formulating of unambiguous questions
- — Proper presentation of questions with reference to stress and facial expressions.

(b) Framing questioning with reference to hierarchical objectives

- — Suitability of different types of questions for various objectives
- — Formulate questions on different categories of objectives

(i) Knowledge eliciting information recalling, recognising,

(Mental-Process-Centric) restructuring behaviours

(Knowledgebricks) reproducing

With 'what', 'who', 'when', 'where'

(ii) Comprehension/Understanding

- — To see relationship and differentiate between various types of information (Mental-Process-Centric behaviours)
- — Seeing relationships
- — Classifying, distinguishing
- — Interpreting, detecting errors, verifying, generalising etc. The basis of framing questions:
- — Reasoning
- — Formulating and establishing hypothesis,
- — Inferring, predicting etc.
- — To arouse thinking of cause and effect-relationship

(c) Presentation and distribution of question on the whole class and feedback through verbal and non-verbal cues.

II. Discussion Initiating, Sustaining and Guiding a Discussion

- — Concluding a discussion

III. Problem Solving

(a) Presentation of a problem

(b) Analysis of the problem

(c) Initiating and sustaining the process of problem solving
(d) Guiding problem solving activities.

IV. Skills for Use of Teaching Aids

(a) Selection of teaching aids as per needs
(b) Preparation of charts, models, maps and diagrams
(c) Operation of mechanical aids
(d) Positioning while writing on and explaining from the blackboard
(e) Writing on the blackboard with reference to size, shape, boldness and colour of letters
(f) Drawing, sketching, preparing tables and graphs on the blackboard.

V. Skills for Aptitude and Behaviour Modification

(a) Patient listening
(b) Suggesting
(c) Guiding
(d) Counseling

3

GUIDELINES FOR TEACHER TRAINEES/INTERNS

Record the Course Content

Get a copy of the syllabus, and record the content of the syllabus which you are supposed to cover in the class during the whole session.

Plan the Course

(i) Find out how many class periods will be available to you for the whole course.
(ii) List the units to be covered.
(iii) Analyse the units into topics to give an idea of the scope of the course.
(iv) Arrange the units in a sequence that you think, will be the most effective. (The sequence in the textbooks may not be effective from the point of view of classroom teaching, so change it.)
(v) Allocate the available number of periods to various units, keeping in view the requirements of each unit.

Plan the Teaching Unit

(i) List the goals (general objectives) of the unit,
(ii) List the topics to be covered in the unit,
(iii) Analyse the topics into teaching-points to give an idea of the scope of the unit. Don't limit yourself to the textbook only for this, consult some other standard books and journals on the topic/subject.

(iv) Arrange the topics in a sequence that you think will be most effective. (Avoid the textbook sequence and base it on your experiences and the students' background).

(v) List the teaching aids that you intend using in a topic,

(vi) Include, if possible some activity/excursion/field trip etc., within the sequence,

(vii) Allocate the periods to each topic in the unit. Remember that the total number of periods for the unit has already been decided in the course-plan. Also remember that one or two class periods have to be kept aside for unit-test or evaluation.

(viii) If a topic is allotted more than one period, divide it into class-lessons and decide the sequence of the lessons.

(ix) Finalise the plan of each unit for each day lesson before you start teaching the unit.

Plan the Lesson

A. *Know the Context*

Record the context of the lesson—to which unit it belongs and at which serial number it appears in the Unit-Plan.

B. *Define the Objectives*

List instructional objectives of the lesson.

Remember that the teaching fails if the teacher is not clear about the objectives.

While writing objectives, remember that—

(i) Objectives should state specific content and specific pupil-behaviour, i.e., what the students would be able to do after the lesson is over.
Such objectives always contain one specific active verb for the pupil, e.g., Pupils define/list/compare . . . . . .

(ii) Objectives should not be limited to memory-actions (define, list, describe, draw, identify)
But should cover Higher-Order Thinking actions also, e.g., Pupils distinguish/use analyse/modify/estimate/generalize/review/evaluate . . . . .

(iii) Objectives relating to the development of skills, interest and attitudes should be included also, e.g.

Skills

Pupils draw (map or diagram or figure)/set/handle (the apparatus)/fold/ out/prepare/collect—

Interest and Attitude

Pupils collect (specimens/poems etc.)/memorise (poem)/praise (a painting of their choice)/interview)

C. *Define Previous Knowledge Required*

Analyse the previous knowledge assumed, i.e., list the skills, fact or principles which the pupils are supposed to know for learning the new lesson, e.g., to learn to multiply 2-digit numbers, the pupils must be able to add, and to count upto 100.

Remember, if our assumptions about the previous knowledge of the class are wrong, the teaching would fail.

D. *Plan The Teaching Aids*

Mention the teaching aids that you intend using in the lesson.

Remember, blackboard, duster and chalk are treated as essentials and therefore not mentioned.

E. *Plan the Introduction*

The purpose of Introduction is a lesson-plan is to motivate the students to participate in learning the new lesson. This is done by recalling their previous experiences to lead them to the lesson, through various techniques viz.

(a) brief narration or recitation by the teacher
(b) pointing to and reading an item from a newspaper or a magazine or a poster etc.
(c) asking questions to test the previous knowledge essential to learn the lesson
(d) asking questions to initiate the discussion based on their previous experiences.

The effectiveness of Introduction depends much on the imaginativeness of the teacher. New techniques may be invented. At least, the same technique should not be repeated everyday.

F. *Plan the Presentation*

1. *Teaching points*
While planning teaching points, see that the—

   (a) Teaching points cover all the specific objectives of the lesson (e.g., in language lessons it generally happens that the entire lesson stresses the comprehension aspect alone, ignoring other objective of language development).
   (b) Teaching points are sufficient to engage the full lesson-period as well as not so many to render the lesson incomplete, (This requires that the teacher knows the ability level of his class and plans the pace of the lesson.)
   (c) Teaching points are indicative of the teachers' mastery of the subject also. The teacher should not limit therefore to the textbook only for planning the lesson, rather should consult a number of standard books and journals on the subject.
   (d) An appropriate sequence is decided.

2. *Teacher Activity*
After deciding the teaching points and their sequence, think—which activities you can initiate for each. Various activities are:

reading,
explaining,
illustrating with examples,
questioning,
asking students to make questions,
discussing with the help of an aid demonstrating,
sketching on the blackboard and discussing,
summarizing/solving on the blackboard,
giving practice,
asking students to work in groups and so on,
Specify the activities that you plan to use for each point.

3. *Pupil activity*
In response to your activities, the pupils are expected to say or do something. Write specially, what they are expected to say or do.

G. *Plan Recapitulation/Evaluation*

Recapitulation is to review the whole lesson briefly so that the points are fixed and organized in memory. Evaluation is to assess to what extent the learning has taken place. Questioning, once again, is the technique employed for these purposes. Make it a point that

— questions are asked only about the content which has been discussed
— blackboard should be cleared and aids (charts etc.) be removed before recapitulation/evaluation
— every point can not be covered. Focus questions on main points only.
— objective type or short-answer type questioning are helpful.

H. *Plan Home Assignment*

— Assign home-work which the pupils can do on the basis of their class-learning and they do not need the help of parents etc. Remember, most of the pupils come from illiterate and/or busy homes.
— Assign work which may give practice (with summary, diagram solving questions) extend learning (interview, extra reading) develop interest in learning (collect specimens etc.)
— Assign as much work as you can check conveniently. It is better not to give assignment than to leave it unchecked.
— Keep individual differences in assignment. Make assignment flexible, for example:
Write summary or interpretation or examples, solve at least five questions.
— Assign creative and imaginative work also sometimes.

While You are Actually Teaching

You have planned many teacher activities in your lesson plan. Each activity needs many points to remember and practice. Below are some suggestions regarding some important activities:

A. *Explaining*

1. Make a beginning state before actual explaining to attract attention.

2. Use explaining links like 'because-therefore', 'when-then'
3. Make a concluding statement after the explanation to review the main points or to indicate just that the explanation is over.
4. Ask questions to test whether the pupils have understood the explanation. Do not just ask 'Have you understood?' Ask specific questions.
5. Use vocabulary according to the level of the students. Do not use very difficult words and very complex sentences, simplify.
6. Take care of the speed and voice the explanation is intelligible.
7. Avoid vague and irrelevant statements.

B. *Illustrating With Examples*

1. Use both verbal and non-verbal illustrations.
2. Give sufficient number of examples.
3. See that the examples are relevant and interesting.
4. Invite students to give examples of variety.
5. Organise examples appropriately—either in the beginning to lead to a generalization or after the interpretation of the principle.
6. Use media according to the level of pupil understanding.

C. *Questioning*

1. Questions may be used to initiate a point to develop the discussion or to test the knowledge. Be aware of your purpose. Questions should not be asked just for the sake of questions.
2. Questions should be structured correctly i.e. see that your questions are:
   — relevant (to your purpose)
   — specific (to the point)
   — concise (without superfluous words like 'will your tell . . .')
   — correct grammatically.
3. Questioning becomes successful if the following points are kept in mind:

   (i) Avoid questions of 'yes', 'no' type.
   (ii) Avoid using the words of the text in questions.
   (iii) Avoid asking the questions in the line-to-line sequence of the text.

(iv) Ask questions pertaining to each objective. For example, in language-lesson, do not restrict to understanding of the content, do ask questions about linguistic, and style features.

(v) Ask questions to stimulate thinking, to interpret, to discuss, to elaborate, to compare, to criticise, to judge.

(vi) Ask divergent questions also, with various acceptable answers. Ask them to suggest, to illustrate, to give example, to modify. Imaginative questions also may be asked—'what would happen . . . . .', or 'what would you do if you . . . . '

4. Some psychological points may also be kept in mind:
   (i) Avoid naming a student before asking the question. Pose the question to whole class and then ask particular students.
   (ii) Do not be impatient. Give them time to think. Do not give the answer yourself.
   (iii) Involve the maximum number of students through questioning. Ask those also who do not raise hands—they may be shy only.

D. *Dealing with Pupil Responses*

A question asked may result in any of the following type of responses from pupils:

no response
incorrect response
partially correct response
incomplete response
correct response.

Any response has to be dealt in two ways—one psychologically, the other conceptually.

Psychologically

(i) avoid punishing the response. The pupils may otherwise tend to withdraw and not respond at all.

(ii) reward good, desirable response so that pupils are encouraged to give responses.

Conceptually, many strategies can be adopted.

1. in case of no-response,

— encourage to answer
— revise the question in simpler words
— break the question into parts and ask simple questions, give an example or a hint and ask the question.

2. in case of incorrect answer
   — ask to reconsider.
   — give a hint or an example and ask to revise.
   — discuss by breaking the question into parts.
3. in case of partially correct or incomplete response,
   — accept the correct part and ask to reconsider the incorrect/ incomplete part.
   — discuss the incorrect part by breaking the original question into parts, by asking questions to get further information.
   — redirect question to other pupils to have a discussion.
4. in case of correct response,
   — reward the response appropriately.
   — ask the pupil to elaborate further, or to give example or to illustrate.
   — ask for more complex information.
   — ask to give reasons or to justify.
   — redirect to other pupils for elaboration and discussion

E. *Providing Practice/Drill*

On occasions, practice and drill become necessary in the classroom, for example, in pronunciation in language, in using symbols in mathematics, in reading/preparing map, in sketching or recording readings in science. While giving practice

— move through the class,
— watch the performance of the students,
— guide individually when asked and when you feel that the pupil needs help,
— invite fast learners to guide other students with you if a large number of students need help.

F. *Using Blackboard*

— See that your handwriting is legible. If not, practise it.
— Use blackboard:

to focus on main points,
to sketch and discuss,
to solve a problem.

— Avoid using blackboard to give lengthy notes or solving all problems.
— Have a visual image in your mind what you are going to write on the blackboard and use it appropriately, then your blackboard work will become neat and organized.
— involve students also in blackboard work, if possible.
— Write date, class, subject, topic on the top corner of the blackboard. If the board is very small, erase it when needed.
— Clean the blackboard before leaving the class.

G. *Using Aids/Demonstrations*

— Blackboard chalk, duster are common place and essential. Do not mention them.
— Use aids with a purpose. Do not use just for using them.
— Do not give everything in the aid. Leave something for the students to think and discuss.
— Exhibit the aid that it is observable to all.
— After exhibiting, ask the students to observe, to concentrate and then to report their observations, to comment, to discuss, to suggest. Avoid explaining yourself.
— If the demonstration fails, or there is some flaw in the aid, ask the students to hypothesis, to comment and to discuss. Do not get confused.

H. *Providing Better Climate*

— Encourage the students to speak out what they think or feel.
— Be friendly and sympathetic.
— Avoid comparing students with one-another.
— Be firm, but not harsh, or offending.

Expectations from Interns/Trainees

The trainees are required—

During the Internship

1. to teach about 20 lessons in each of their two subjects in a

planned manner, preparing unit-plans, whenever required and lesson plans each day;
2. to observe ten lessons of co-trainees on the schedule provided by the college (at least two observations must be made of any trainee);
3. to assess their own teaching at least once through unit-test in either subject after a unit is completed;
4. to use teaching aids in their lessons, and construct at least one;
5. to conduct school-activity other than teaching whether register work or student activity;
6. to complete other assignments required by the college departments;
7. to participate fully in the routine school work including Examinations, Co-curricular Programmes Remedial Classes or Parent-Teacher Meetings. (Arrangement classes are also included under this experience but may be avoided during the first week).
8. to learn to work and behave as teachers under the guidance of cooperating teachers.

Specifically, it is advised that—

Daily

1. They attend the school punctually and stay full time as the school timings demand, (only 2 day's casual leave in the whole Internship Programme is permissible on genuine grounds, and by the school principal, not the college supervisors);
2. They sign the attendance register at the time of arrival and departure;
3. They get their lesson plans checked and signed by their cooperating teachers before the lessons are taught;
4. They write their lesson-diary and daily-diary provided by the college;

On the First Day

1. They report to the principal of the school they are allotted for internship;
2. They get classes allotted to them in their subjects of teaching;

3. They consult their cooperating teachers about the courses they shall be expected to teach in the classes;
4. They prepare Unit Plan for teaching-subject from the next (second) day;
5. They prepare their first Lesson Plan according to the unit/plan for the second day;

On the Second Day

1. They show the unit plan and lesson-plan to the concerned cooperating teacher and get them signed;
2. They teach the first lesson;
3. They prepare Unit Plan in the second subject;
4. They prepare lesson-plans in both the subjects to be taught in the next (third) day;

During the First Week

1. They get themselves allotted classes and other school-assignments.

During the Second Week

1. They start 'observation' of lessons of co-trainees;
2. They start working on other college-assignments;

During the Fifth/Sixth Week

1. They specially prepare for and teach 'Final Lesson'.

Related Experiences for Student Teacher/Intern

The list of related experiences given below is not suggested as a basis for any particular assigned activity. It is simply to give the Interns some guidance toward an understanding of the varied aspects of the operation of any school, with its internal and external relationships and procedures identified to aid their understanding of their multiplicity and variety.

1. *Administration*
   (a) Who are the people involved?

(b) What are the chief duties of these offices?
(c) What responsibilities have teachers to these offices?

2. *School Facilities*
(a) What is the general physical "lay out"?
(b) What recreation or playground facilities?
(c) How is the auditorium used?
(d) How is the cafeteria operated?
(e) What provision is made for teachers' lounges?
(f) What duplicating facilities are available?

3. *Curriculum*
(a) General "overall" purpose of programme of studies?
(b) What are the basic required courses?
(c) If practiced, what is basis of grouping?
(d) What are trends in elective courses?
(e) What provision is made for "gifted" students?
(f) What remedial work is offered?

4. *Library*
(a) How is library staffed?
(b) What services does the library over to classroom teachers?
(c) How do class groups use the library?

5. *Equipment and Materials*
(a) How are textbooks handled?
(b) What visual aids equipment is available?
(c) How are visual aids provided?
(d) How are teaching supplied obtained?

6. *Guidance*
(a) What personnel is involved?
(b) What student records are maintained?
(c) What test procedures are used?
(d) What standardized tests are given?
(e) How is the guidance programme organized?
(f) Are student graduate "follow-ups" made?
(g) What orientation for the incoming students is provided?
(h) How to extra-class activities relate to guidance?
(i) By whom are students' programmes made?

7. *Health Services*
   (a) Is a clinic maintained?
   (b) How is it staffed?
   (c) What examinations are given?
   (d) What health services are provided?
   (e) What is relation to city health and social agencies?

8. *Grading and Reporting*
   (a) How are standardized test scores used?
   (b) How are grades determined?
   (c) How are grades reported?
   (d) Is provision made for parents' conferences?

9. *Extra-Class Activities*
   (a) On what is participation based?
   (b) What limitations are placed on participants?
   (c) What recognition is given to participants?
   (d) How are such activities financed?
   (e) What is their relation to other schools?
   (f) What is their relation to the community?
   (g) Is there a home room programme?

10. *Student Government*
   (a) What student body organizations exists?
   (b) How do they function in relation to the school programme?
   (c) How is leadership recognized?
   (d) Responsibility is accepted for what activities?

11. *Community Resources*
   (a) What community agencies maintain active contacts?
   (b) What parent groups function?
   (c) How is communication maintained with parents and community?
   (d) What "special" events promote contacts?

12. *Professional Groups*
   (a) Frequency and nature of faculty meetings?
   (b) What "in-service activities"?
   (c) What consulting services are available?
   (d) Where are such persons or agencies located?
   (e) Membership is available in what organizations?

Something More

For the most part more responsible behaviour and closer application to the job at hand is expected from each student teacher than has been true in any previous college course. Most student teachers are painstaking about their work for they are aware of the implications of lack of success in their student teaching. They are further motivated by the realization that they may soon be applying for a position and that success in student teaching is one solid measure for reference in seeking employment. Observation of certain "high points" will make their experience not only much more pleasant, but also will contribute markedly to their success:

Dear Trainees

1. You should be dependable and punctual. Report on time for each day's work, and if you are ill call the school office and ask that your supervising teacher be notified.
2. Prepare carefully and in detail for each day. It is not enough to be ready to "stand and deliver" on schedule. You should be prepared for any emergency which may arise.
3. Learn names of all pupils as quickly as possible. The teacher-student relationship, if sound, contributes most to successful teaching. Avoid being too "chummy" with the students.
4. Abide by all regulations which apply to students and to teachers. You are not a visitor in a privileged status, but a fellow worker subject to established standards.
5. Expect to give more assistance than you receive. Expect and event ask to be allowed to participate in all duties: playground, lunchroom, clubs, field trips, etc.
6. You are obligated to know your pupils are completely as possible through observation, conferences, and examination of test scores and school records.
7. In the classroom, try to avoid seeming to either "take over" or materially change procedures. Remember the practical seldom approximates the theoretical. This is not the quarter to revise the school programme.
8. Assume responsibility for or help with the physical conditions of the room: light, heat, ventilation, equipment, and supplementary materials.

9. Quickly find your way about so that you become acquainted with the school plant (and custodian), the administration and its organization and functioning, routines for reporting, etc.
10. Be as "professional" as any member of the permanent staff of the school. There is no reason during your teaching assignment for criticism of teachers, the administration, the school-facilities, or any other related phase of the school-operation. Avoid discussion of personalities.
11. College activities should not be allowed to interfere with the time devoted to student teaching. Your sense of values should guide you in the division of your time and attention. Avoid credit hour overload.
12. You may be expected, as is any teacher, to give such extra time as may be needed in helping the students solve their problems, and in participation in extra class activities.
13. A strong sense of the "rightness" of things is necessary. If teachers do not smoke, or the community disapproves, then you should not. Dress appropriately—as other teaches do in your school. Avoid high heels, sneakers, sport shirts, tight sweaters, clashing colours.
14. Have a receptive attitude toward suggestion and criticism. If errors are to be avoided and/or corrected such an attitude must exist, based upon recognition of the concern for a job well done by all personnel participating.

Experiences for the Student Teacher/Intern

The following list is simply suggestive and is not intended to be all-inclusive, nor are the items listed in order of importance. Your supervising teacher will make his own selection of experiences appropriate to your situation, in line with your indicated ability and interest. However, it is suggested that you should seek, and have, all of the following experiences.

1. Study the pupils' cumulative record folders.
2. Prepare and use a seating chart.
3. Plan and teach a unit or units.
4. Construct, administer and score tests.
5. Teach in as many phases of the major and/or minor field as is consistent with your supervisor's long-range plans.

6. Learn to use all available audio-visual equipment.
7. Learn to use all available duplicating equipment.
8. Attend P.T.A. and school athletic or social functions.
9. Supervise a study hall.
10. Be responsible for assisting pupils with make-up work.
11. Requisition and account for school supplies.
12. Make child studies or systematic observation reports.
13. Help a class to plan and to develop a school assembly programme.
14. Make arrangements for a field trip or an outside speaker.
15. Cooperate in noon lunch hour supervision.
16. Assist in carrying out fire or civil defense drill.
17. Utilize the school library facilities.
18. Supervise pupils before and after school or do "bus" duty.
19. Help with the standardized testing programme.
20. Supervise the proper care of science or other equipment.
21. Assist with co-curricular or other clubs.
22. Help with approved fund or school "drives".
23. Arrange bulletin board or other display materials.
24. Conduct an individual student conference.
25. Develop experience in teacher-pupil planning.
26. Select and send for suitable free instructional materials.

Guidelines for Cooperating Teachers/Principals

Internship in teaching is a special method of teacher-training which places the trainee in the learning environment of the school on full time basis. The training is required to learn the job of a teacher, not simply the method of teaching a class. For the purpose, he/she is entrusted to the guidance of regular teacher(s) who help him/her develop the competencies of a teacher. Naturally, the regular teacher plays a crucial role since it is she/he who demonstrates to the trainee how to teach and conduct various school jobs.

The trainees are supposed to teach in a planned manner as the regular teachers do (they may not write 'lesson plans' but they do have 'mental plan' of the lesson). Besides the trainees are expected to complete several other assignments. The cooperative teacher can help to trainees in the following manner.

1. Accept the trainee as *apprentice*, introduce him/her to the class, intimate the course he/she is supposed to teach.

2. Guide him/her in preparing the unit plan and the lesson plans; checking the lesson plan *each day* before it is actually taught. Be strict that the trainee comes prepared daily. any default may be treated seriously.
3. Encourage him/her for using teaching aids (concrete materials) to make lesson more effective and interesting; help him/her guide to prepare own materials.
4. *Encourage* him/her for using *activity method*. It is required more so with trainees for B.Ed. (Ele. Edn.) teaching younger children. The trainees may use activity in the classroom, outside the class in the school or outside the school if it could be managed. The cooperation and guidance by the regular teacher is essential in this regard.
5. Guide the trainee in planning and conduction of a *unit test* advice him/her to diagnose the weaknesses of students and then provide them individual or group guidance.
6. Assess his/her teaching in the class personally. The college supervisors do visit to observe but it is the cooperating teacher who is a regular observer of the growth of the trainee, and therefore, the most effective person to guide him/her. In order, to assess the development, the teacher-guide is required to:

   (i) observe the class teaching daily and record comments/ suggestions in the supervision notebook;
   (ii) *especially* observe the *first lesson* and *Criticism Lesson* during third/fourth week and *grade/mark* the performance on various aspects of teaching. (The grades/marks for all the trainees are to be consolidated at the school level.)
   (iii) *assess* the teaching performance of the trainees on overall basis at the end of internship in the subject of teaching.

   Please Note that *distinction* level (75 per cent or above) or first class marks (60 to 75 per cent) are given *only when* the performance is really extra-ordinary or first class level. Pass percentage is 40 percent and second division from 50 to 60 per cent.

7. Discuss freely and frankly, but not in a discouraging manner, with the trainee his/her teaching-performance. If it is felt that a demonstration lesson may help the trainee to improve,

demonstration may be given. It is most welcome.

8. Sometime, other trainees may be observing the lesson of the trainee entrusted to you. *Encourage* the observers also for discussion after the lesson is finished in your spare time guiding them *how to observe and record. Encourage* your apprentice for self-evaluation his/her own performance. Check their observations and sign the observation schedule.
9. Guide the trainee in doing his/her *school assignments.*
10. *Provide* administrative help to the trainee in data collection for college assignments;
11. Advise the trainee to participate in the school programmes with enthusiasm.
12. Share experiences with the college supervisors freely and frankly when they visit schools during the internship, the trainee is more an apprentice than college student.

Expectations from Cooperating Schools

— To get the interns introduced with school staff, students, surroundings and working.

— To get them adjusted with the new environment of school and its academic work.

— To help them in lodging and boarding. If the school has hostel the interns may kindly be accommodated there, if possible.

— To allot the interns classes as per their teaching subjects. It would be better if in one period not more than two or three interns are allotted classes so that there may be proper supervision.

— To provide a room for interns in the school, if possible, for sitting, discussion and preparation.

— To request the cooperating teachers/subject teachers to supervise the interns and improve their teaching.

— Subject teachers act as their mentor.

— To request the subject teachers to help and improve the lesson plans.

— To provide the available teaching aids to interns for various subjects they are teaching.

— To help and guide the internees in preparation and suitable use of teaching aids.

— To help, guide and provide facilities to interns for experiments, demonstration, practical lessons and activity lessons etc.

— To request the subject teachers to give demonstration lessons where necessary.

— To provide the experience of arranging educational excussion/ field trip, if possible.

— To associate the interns in all the activities of the school such as prayer, sports and games, cultural activities, other co-curricular activities of the school and school examinations.

— To train them in maintaining registers, fee collection and the like responsibilities expected from a teacher.

— To guide and help them in completing their assignments to be completed during the internship.

— To co-operate with the training college staff supervisors in completing internship programme.

— To send the marks of each intern evaluated on the basis of their total performance during internship.

Headmaster/Headmistress/Principal/Controlling officer of interns during the internship and cooperating teachers/subject teachers are their friend, philosopher and guide.

4

ASSIGNMENTS

Alongwith teaching, the trainees/interns should be provided all the relevant experiences related to the job of a teacher. During Pre-Internship phases they should be thoroughly oriented for related assignments related tools should be developed and provided to trainees. Care should be taken that these assignments are quite practical, activity-oriented and useful for the teacher. The Interns/trainees will complete the assignments and submit the same at the time of viva-voce during Post-Internship Phase.

Guidelines for some assignments are suggested here. The teacher-educator and training-college faculty have to decide which and how many assignments should be assigned to the trainees.

ASSIGNMENT 1

SCHOOL CALENDAR

School Calender is a register maintained by every school and contains information about all the activities to be undertaken by the school during an academic session.

The register contains different items of work/activities to be undertaken by the school alongwith the dates by which these activities or work should normally be completed.

School Calender helps the school to conduct its different activities in an organised manner and also eliminate chances of any lapses on the part of the school. The register serves as a kind of a reminder, a 'memory tickler' to the school administration.

The register contains items such as follows:

	Events	*Date*
1.	Admissions	
2.	Preparation of Time-Table	
3.	Conduct of Examinations	

Events	*Date*
4. Declaration of Results	
5. Celebration of different festivals.	
6. Observation of Independence Day. Republic Day Celebrations.	
7. Organisations of picnics and excursions for different classes.	
8. Organisation of sports weeks, sports meets etc.	
9. Annual celebrations.	
10. Account of vacations.	

While writing an assignment on school calender, you may yourself maintain a register and complete the entries during an academic session and then write an analytical report on the same. While writing the report you may keep the following in mind:

1. Do the activities undertaken by the school show a certain organised manner of doing things?
2. Have the dates fixed for doing different activities by the schools been adhered to?
3. Could some more activities have been undertaken by the school which would have proved beneficial to the students and for which sufficient time and facilities were available.
4. Suggestions for improvement, if any.

ASSIGNMENT 2

ANALYSIS OF A TEXTBOOK

A textbook serves an avowed instructional purpose—dissemination of information and knowledge in a graded and sequential manner. That it plays a major role in the total process of teaching and learning, need not be emphasised here.

Whether the textbook serves the purpose for which it was written can be evaluated by following a pattern of evaluation for the textbooks.

Select a textbook prescribed for students of your school in any subject, preferably your teaching subject, and evaluate it to find out whether it really serves the avowed purpose.

The following principles may be kept in mind while evaluating a textbook.

A. *Contents*

1. What is the place of the subject in the school curriculum?
   (a) Compulsory
   (b) Subsidiary
2. What are the objectives of teaching the subject?
3. What is the relative importance given to each of these objectives?
   (a) in teaching in the classroom.
   (b) in the examination.
4. For whom is the textbook written? Does the author clearly specify it?
   (a) Age level
   (b) Grade level.
5. Does the textbook help in realising the objectives of teaching the subject?
   (a) if it helps, how?
   (b) if it does not help, why?
6. Are the topics/contents in the textbook related to the objectives of teaching the subject?
7. To what extent is the distribution of the contents of the book proportional to the importance of the objectives of teaching the subject?
8. How many pages does the book contain? How are these pages distributed over each of the contents/topics in the book?
9. How are the contents/topics organised?
   (a) Graded
   (b) Ungraded
   (c) Mixed up
10. Treatment of Topics/Contents
    A. To what extent does it provide opportunity to children:
       (a) to learn at their own rate?
       (b) the chance to repeat or review?
       (c) possibility for checking for recall?
       (d) the case with which notes may be made for later use?
    B. How far the illustrations, graphs, pictures and chart (if any) help to elucidate the subject matter in the book?
       (a) Are they relevant?
       (b) Irrelevant?
       (c) Superfluous?

Do these illustrations appear at the place they should be?
If yes, how do you justify them?
If no, what places would you suggest for them?

B. Is the Language (words, sentences, syntactical elements, relevant terms)
   (a) easy to understand?
   (b) Does it help to develop and sustain interest?
   (c) Does it possess qualities favourable to success by the students.

C. Does the text book help in providing continuity, precision, order, and proportion in the school programme?

B. *Format*

(a) Is the general format of the book attractive and suitable for the age/grade/level for which it has been written?
(b) Are the following suitably adjusted for better readability.
   1. Type of the page.
   2. Size of the line.
   3. Length of the line.
   4. Interlined space.
   5. Margin.
   6. Width of type and boldness of stroke.
   7. Colour of ink and quality and colour of paper.
   8. Binding.

Analytical Report

After you have examined a textbook from the above mentioned angles, write a comprehensive report analysing the textbook as a whole. You may include any other aspects for the evaluation of a textbook, not included in the tool and which are relevant to the textbook in question.

ASSIGNMENT 3

ANALYSIS OF A QUESTION PAPER

Question papers/for examination play an important role in the process of education. They help us in the evaluation of child's achievement. But in order to help us properly to evaluate the child's achievement, a question paper must be complete in all respects and should follow a pattern so that functions attached to a question paper are performed adequately.

In order to evaluate a question paper the following criteria may be followed:

1. *Introductory information about the Question Paper*
   Name of the School/Board, Class, Subject, Paper No./Code, Time allotted, Maximum Marks, Total No. of Questions, No. of Questions to be attempted, Instructions to the examinees.
2. *Clarity of instructions*
   Are the instructions clear and continuous? Are these instructions given in simple language?
3. *Content coverage*
   Does the examination-paper cover the prescribed topics in the syllabus?
   List the topics left out.
4. *Objectives*
   To what extent does the question paper attempt to evaluate the objectives of teaching the subject, i.e.
   (i) Knowledge
   (ii) Understanding
   (iii) Application and skill.
5. *Distribution of question according to their objectives*
   (a) Number of knowledge-testing questions.
   (b) Number of comprehension-testing questions.
   (c) Number of skill-testing questions.
   (d) Number of questions testing originality of the students.
6. *Forms of questions*
   (a) No. of objective type
   (b) No. of short answer type
   (c) No. of essay type
7. *Order of the question*
   Are the questions arranged in the order of difficulty level? Examine the nature of the questions whether they require explanation or description or critical analysis of the subject matter.
8. *Language*
   Is the language of the questions adequately simple? Examine if the students are not likely to suffer due to ambiguity or difficulty of language.
9. *Meeting the individual levels*
   Does the question paper contain enough questions for all types

(i.e. bright, average, below average) of students. Is the question paper stimulating and challanging?

10. *Distribution of marks, objectivity and ease in scoring*
    Is the distribution of marks over questions and parts of questions (if any) given?
    Can the answers of students be evaluated with sufficient ease and accuracy?
11. *Strong points of the question paper*
12. *Errors or other discrepancies?*
    Are there any factual errors? Does the question paper suffer from discripencies?
13. *Limitation of the question paper*
14. *Other aspects of the question paper*
    (a) Printing errors
    (b) type used
    (c) quality of paper
    (d) arrangement of questions according to difficulty level.
15. *Suggestions for improvement* : ______________________________
16. *Analytical report*:
    After you have examined a question paper for the above mentioned aspects, write a comprehensive report analysing the question paper as a whole. A reasonably good report can be given in two or three pages. You may include any other aspect for the evaluation of a question paper. The above mentioned format is merely a suggestive list of certain aspects of a good question paper.

ASSIGNMENT 4

PRACTICAL ASSIGNMENT IN SOCIOMETRY

The Sociometry is a technique for describing social relations that exist between individuals in a group. It is a method to describe attractions or repulsions between individuals by asking them to indicate as to whom they would choose or reject in various situations. Children in a class room may be asked to name a child or several other children in order of preference that they would invite to a party, eat lunch with, sit next to, in the class, work on a class project or go on a educational excursion. Sociometric studies have been made on classroom groups, camp groups, factory and office groups and on members of the armed forces for spotting out leadership qualities of the members. These most often chosen individuals are called *Stars* and those who are rejected are called *Isolates*.

There may be a third group of individuals who choose one another. They are called Cliques. The Sociometry is a useful technique for knowing whether or not a group has established satisfying social relationships.

Problem

You may conduct a Sociometric Study on students of either IX, or X or XI classes by asking them the following three questions:

1. Name the student with whom you would like to do your home work.
2. Name the student with whom you would like to work on class project.
3. Name the student with whom you would like to garden class project.

Ask the students to write their preferences on a piece of paper and keep it confidential. Count the votes secured by each student. You may then sketch the sociogram, by writing the roll numbers of the students and encircle the role numbers of the candidates who were getting maximum votes.

Example

Given below is a Sociogram indicating that the students with Role Nos. 6, 10 and 14 received the highest number of votes from classmates for the above mentioned three activities.

SOCIOGRAM

1	2	3	4	5
6	7	8	9	10
11	12	13	14	15
16	17	18	19	20

Now prepare a list on the basis of your own study in rank order indicating the votes obtained by the students in each of the three activities:

1. Who were the most liked students?

2. Are the students for the three activities different?
3. Were there any students who did not receive a single vote?

Write a brief report giving answers to the above mentioned questions.

ASSIGNMENT 5

CUMULATIVE RECORD CARD

Cumulative record usually represents an attempt to collect certain basic information about a student in a school and to which data are added as they are accumulated. Usually the information collected about the student relates to various areas such as, identification data, home background, health record, academic record, educational plans, vocational interests etc.

If your school is maintaining such a record, use the same and collect data about five students separately and interpret the record and give a summary of your findings in the form of a report.

In case your school is not maintaining any Cumulative Record you may develop one of your own under the following heads and collect information about 3 students on the given outlines.

(a) Identifying Data (name, age, class, family background)

- (i) Academic Record
- (ii) Physical Data give description about the nature of the health of the students.
- (iii) Personality Traits. Mention here leadership qualities and adjustment to the school, participation in co-curricular activities etc.
- (iv) Educational and Vocational Plans or Future.
- (v) Summary: give your own interpretation of the students' academic achievement, personality traits, and his participation in co-curricular activities etc.

ASSIGNMENT 6

ACTION RESEARCH

In the case of action research, the person faces a problem and tries to find out its solution by researching in a scientific way through different lines of action.

When a teacher faces a problem in the classroom he does a number of things. Firstly he thinks about the nature of the problem and tries to visualise it is proper perspective. He then thinks of the ways and means of solving the problem. A number of solutions come to his mind in the hypothetical form. He proceeds to take action on his hypothesis to test whether his hypothesis or conception of a line of action for the solution of the problem is appropriate and worth-while. At times, during the process, he finds that his line of action is not correct for the solution of a problem. He takes resort to another process and so on.

Many good teachers are using action research in their daily lessons without calling it so by name.

In action research a teacher has not to wait for months to see the results of his approach. Here the results are seen immediately during teaching a lesson or immediately after the lesson is over.

Action research is a continuous process which includes the trying out of a line of approach, recording the results, changing the approach— if the desired results are not achieved, adopting a new approach and so on. As such it is a flexible process depending upon the need and conditions of a situation. The teacher has neither to create some artificial conditions nor to disturb the normal class routine to carry on this type of research.

Plan of Action Research

1. Problem Area
2. Pinpointed Problem
3. Causes of the Problem
4. Action Hypothesis
5. Testing of Hypothesis
   A. Data to be collected
   B. Tools procedures to be used
6. Design of the Action Research

ACTION PROCEDURE

S. No.	Date		Plan of Work	Tools to be used
	From	To		
1.				
2.				
3.				
4.				
5.				
6.				

Conclusions

The method of collecting data shall be repeated to find out the difference among the pupils, before and after the experimentation. Conclusions shall be drawn on the basis of the collected, data.

Follow up

In the selection of problems trainees should not take the problem of Late Comings as sufficient work has already been done on it.

Write the Action Research Report: It should be written in clear and simple language on the following lines:

1. Title of the project
   (i) The problems area
   (ii) The pin-pointed problem
2. Objectives of the Research:
   (i) Significance of the problem
   (ii) Purpose of the study
   (iii) Diagnosis of the problem
   (iv) The Action hypothesis
3. Design of the Study or Action Plan:
   (i) Procedure adopted
   (ii) Sources of data
   (iii) Methods of gathering data
   (iv) Main findings
   (v) Action taken to solve the problem.
4. Evaluation of the Project:
   (i) Methods employed for evaluation
   (ii) Definite and significant changes
   (iii) Lead for another plan or recommendations for further Action Research

ASSIGNMENT 7

CASE STUDY

The trainee may select an average, gifted, backward or a student having some behaviour problem for making a case study. A proforma for making a case study of backward student is given. The proforma may be modified, if necessary. Proforma for making case study of an average or a gifted student may be developed by the candidate on similar lines. The main difference here will be that the focus will shift from diagnosing the cause of backwardness to study of positive achievements. At the same time it is to be kept in mind, that no one is without problems and all of us have unutilized potential for greater achievements. Suggestions for further improvement can be given for the average as well as the gifted student.

Proforma for Making a Case Study of a Backward Student

(The main emphasis in the proforma is on the possible cause of backwardness.)

1. *Preliminary Data*
   Name, age, class, socio-economic status.
2. *Physical Condition*
   Is the health normal or are there some defects present. Some major defects related to backwardness are:

   (i) Defects of the sensory organs : visual, auditory
   (ii) General auditory weakness
   (iii) Speech defects : stammering
   (iv) Specific physical defects

3. *Environmental Influences*
   (i) Home : Relationship with the parents.
      (a) Is there constant discord between the child and the parents?
      (b) Is the child rejected by the parents?
      (c) What interest do the parents take in the education of the child?
      (d) Do the parents demand too high standards?
      (e) What is the attitude of the child towards siblings?
   (ii) School :
      (a) Is he regular in attendance?
      (b) How much interest does he have in school subjects?
      (c) Has he any vocational plans? How far are these vocational plans related to the choice of school subjects?
      (d) How is the relationship with the classmates? Is he popular?
      (e) What is his participation in the co-curricular activities?

Intellectual Status

Use an intelligence test if available, otherwise, get the ratings from teachers on a five point or a seven-point scales.

Study Habits

(i) Are there adequate facilities for study at his home? Does he have some place in the home where he can study without any disturbance? Does he have the books he needs?
(ii) Does he have some regular hours for study?
(iii) Does he complete his home work?
(iv) Does he review what has been taught?
(v) Does he report the difficulties to his teachers?
(vi) Does he use a dictionary?
(vii) Has he acquired the habit of silent reading?

Emotional Adjustments

(i) Does he show tendency to withdraw, such as day dreaming, excessive cinema going, spending excessive time in escapist fiction?
(ii) Does he get easily discouraged? How does he react to praise and blame? How much persistence does he show?
(iii) Does he lack in emotional balance?
(iv) Does he lack in self-confidence?
(v) Does he suffer from anxieties, conflicts?
(vi) Does he have healthy interests and hobbies? What are his reading interests? Does he have any hobbies like stamp or coin collecting?

Study of Specific Weaknesses in the Subject/Subjects

(i) History of backwardness: Was he backward from the very beginning? If backwardness started later, what were the causes? From which class did he show it? What were the marks the student obtained in the last examination?
(ii) Prepare a test to find out whether the student has understood the fundamentals in the subject/subjects in which he is backward.

(iii) Make a study of the errors that the student makes in the tests and home assignments.

(iv) Find out whether the students is weak in spellings, has poor handwriting, does not know fundamentals of arithmetic such as addition, multiplication, decimals etc.

Remedial Programme

Consider the causes being backwardness and on that basis give some suggestions to help the student in overcoming his backwardness. Pay special attention to the specific weaknesses in the school subjects and suggest a remedial programme of instruction.

Action Taken

Describe in brief any action that you took in the light of suggested remedial programme.

Suggestions for the Case Study of a Student Having Behaviour Problems

Select one student who has some behaviour difficulty or problem for case study. The following outline is suggested for making the case study.

(i) Preliminary information about the student including his age, class etc.

(ii) History and origin of the problem, give a brief description of the problem behaviour.

(iii) Health record and educational data.

(iv) Interview with the student: Encourage him to talk about himself, his interests, his problems. Do not blame the student. Do not be hasty in giving advice. Be a sympathetic listener. Try to create a cordial relationship (rapport) with the subject.

(v) Family background: Discuss the problem with the parents. Study their attitude towards the case. How much insight do they have into the problems of the case? What solution have they to offer? Be careful not to blame the parent. Avoid giving impractical suggestions.

(vi) Social behaviour and interests: Observe his behaviour in a natural setting. Interview his classmates. Get the opinion of other teachers.

(vii) Use an intelligence test if available. Determine the IQ.

(viii) Make a list of weakness of the student and his environment.

(ix) Diagnosis and recommendations: Give more importance to positive measures. How can the positive qualities of the subject be further developed?

ASSIGNMENT 8

A STUDY OF COMMON ERRORS IN A SCHOOL SUBJECT

In making a study of common errors, the trainee has first to collect samples of students, and then work in different areas of the subject. He may give certain assignments and tests both objective and essay-type. He may also examine the pupils' note-books for home work. After getting these samples the next step would be to mark each mistake. He may then prepare a chart of mistakes putting them into different categories. A study may also be made as to which are more common mistakes. The last step would be to consider what changes should be effected in the teaching method in order to eliminate these errors.

How to make a study of the errors made by the students in a school subject.

1. Study the written work of every student of your class in the subject.
2. Note his class performances.
3. Locate various mistakes frequently made by the students.
4. Classify and categorise these mistakes, i.e. whether the mistakes are of arithmetical nature or on account of wrong or weak understanding of subject-concepts etc.
5. Arrange for remedial measures so as to remove away these weaknesses.
6. Prepare a report of the study.

ASSIGNMENT 9

SCHOOL AND COMMUNITY RELATIONSHIP

School is a social agency created by the community for its own preparation. School is not an island in itself, cut off from the community. This needs to be clearly understood by the teachers. A proforma has been designed to find out in broad outlines the relationship that actually exists between school and community. The teacher-trainee is required to fill in this proforma and write his interpretations.

1. Is there any relationship between the programme of the school and the educational needs of the community.
2. What are the major employment opportunities in the community for which special training is provided in the school?
3. List any major groups of employment-opportunities which you observed in the community for which no training is provided in the school.
4. What are the areas where mutual cooperation between the school and the community would be beneficial.

ASSIGNMENT 10

STUDY OF EQUIPMENTS AND PHYSICAL FACILITIES

In the total process of education, equipment and physical facilities available play an important part. The availability or lack of them may affect pupils' performance. The proper use of these facilities further helps the process of education.

You may prepare an assignment on this aspect of school-life also. The following guidelines may be helpful in enabling you to write the report.

1. How are the stock-books maintained?
   (a) For consumable articles, and
   (b) Non-consumable articles.
2. Prepare a list of firms which supply the material. What are the points kept in view while purchasing things?
3. Prepare a plan of the subject room/laboratory giving the placement of equipment, laboratory, tables, water and gas arrangement.

4. Is the equipment (furniture, office, supplies, visual aids, apparatus, machines) adequate for the purpose of the course?
5. Is the equipment modern and representative of the type used in industry, the farm, office or laboratory?
6. Study the storing facilities:

   (a) What evidence of planning did you observe in the storage of the major items of equipment?
   (b) What is the provision for storing costly apparatus, electrical goods, acids, poisons, etc.?

7. What evidence of planning for the protection of equipment from damage, loss, and abuse, did you observe?
8. What precautions are used to avoid loss of tools and equipments?
9. What means or methods of reducing waste of materials did you observe?
10. Note down you observations regarding the condition in which tools and equipment are left at the end of the class?
11. Not the presence or absence of first-aid equipment.
12. What system is employed to determine whether a student is or is not permitted to use a given piece of hazardous equipment?
13. What improvement would you suggest on the basis of your study?

ASSIGNMENT 11

PREPARATION OF A SCRAP BOOK

The Scrap Books, as the name indicates, is a book prepared with scrap-material such as pictures, newspaper-cuttings drawings, sketches, cutting from magazines and journals etc. The themes of books should be educational value.

The trainees may prepare a Scrap Book in any of their teaching subjects. While preparing the Scrap Book they should keep in mind that:

1. The contents and materials of the Scrap Book in any of their teaching-subjects are relevant to the subject and reflect a them which is educational beneficial to students.
2. So far as possible some theme unit(s) or project(s) may be

developed and illustrated through the Scrap Book.

3. Credit will be given for original, Creative, aesthetic and effective presentations.

Procedure

Have a theme in your mind. Collect pictures from old discarded magazines. Take an album, paste those craps in a sequential manner which should have some educational bearings. Write captions or titles.

ASSIGNMENT 12

PREPARATION OF TEACHING AIDS

Hearing, seeing, looking and listening are the primary means of human learning. What we see and hear markedly influences our behaviour. Because teaching at its best is the stimulation and direction of learning, what learners look at and listen to are major factors in the effectiveness of learning.

Every-school teacher in order to drive home the knowledge he intends to pass on to the student, would do best using different types of educational aids. The use of aids not only motivates the students but also sustains their interest. Teaching aids are, therefore, a kind of necessity to classroom teaching.

You may also prepare teaching aids for the lessons that you deliver under the guidance of your supervisor.

The teaching aids may be in the form of:

1. Pictures
2. Charts
3. Models
4. Maps
5. Flannel Boards
6. Slides
7. Film Strips
8. Others.

ASSIGNMENT 13

CONSTRUCTION OF AN ACHIEVEMENT TEST

A test is standardised situation that provides an individual with a score. The definition contains two important words: 'Standardisation and Score'. By standarised is meant that all the procedures of testing are stated in advance in such a way that all students are tested with the same question or problems in the same way. A test is standardised only if two tests administrators working independently could obtain the same results with the same group of students.

Some of the most essential ingredients of standardisation are:

1. All students should answer the same question;
2. Instructions should be clear and the same should be given to all the students;
3. No students should be given any advantage which is not given to all the students; and
4. A pre-determined system of scoring should uniformly be applied to the answers of all the students.

The second important term in the definition of a test is 'score'. A score means, a numerical indication of a student's performance. Numerical scores are needed, because of the precision which they provide. Such precision allows us to differentiate between the score of all the students.

Much of the test construction is concerned with these two keywords—standardisation and scoring. To obtain standardisation, a carefully edited set of problems or questions is used. Instructions for taking tests are written out in advance. All necessary materials for taking the test are supplied.

To maintain standardisation, all tests should be given in reasonably comparable environments.

A test serves three major types of functions. These functions are:

1. Assessment
2. Prediction
3. Trait measurement

The assessment-function concerns a direct measure of the effectiveness of performance of the learners at a particular point in time.

An example of the assessment-function is seen when the teacher tests his class for progress in a unit of instruction.

The second function of tests is to predict how individuals will behave in other situations. For example, when tests are used to select students for the college, the major purpose is to forecast how well the students will do when they actually go to the college. If tests are accurate in these predictions, they would be considered valid.

The third function which tests serve is to measure various psychological traits, such as anxiety, dogmatism, acquiescene etc.?

The use of tests as both diagnostic and predictive devices in elementary and secondary schools has increased immensely. These tests enable a teacher to give valid and reliable grades. These tests also motivate and direct students to learn. While constructing an achievement test, the teacher must keep the following in mind:

1. The test is reliable. By reliability we mean the consistency of the measurement of a particular achievement from time to time or from test to test.
2. The test is valid. To the degree the test has relevance and yields reliable scores, it has validity. A valid test of educational achievement is one composed of relevant tasks and yields reliable scores.
3. While constructing the achievement-test the purpose of instrument must be clearly decided.
4. The detailed outline of the content to be included must be made. The statement of purpose and the outline of the content should be discussed with other teachers so as to obtain clarifications and if required, incorporate changes in both the statement of purpose and the outline of content. This will help in modifying, changing, discarding, adding items, in the test.
5. The items are then analysed in terms of statistical requirements for final inclusion in the test.
6. Finally, manuals must be carefully written for the administration, scoring and interpretation of the test.

The basic unit of test-construction is the item and the total test scores are obtained by adding up the item-scores. It should be obvious that the total test can be no better than the items of which it is compounded.

The different types of items that are generally used in achievement test are of the following types:

(a) *True-false*. The most familiar type of objective item is the true-false, where in the student is required to mark a statement either true or false.

(b) *Fill-in*. In the fill-in item the student supplies the one term, name or date which either completes a sentence or answers a question.

(c) *Matching*. In the matching items students are presented with two lists of names or facts or principles. In the blank space provided students are asked to write the letter corresponding to the correct activity on the right.

(d) *Multiple Choice*. In this type of objective items the student is required to choose an alternate response to a problem or question.

Student-trainees may take up construction of an achievement-test in any of the teaching subject they have offered for their degree.

ASSIGNMENT 14

GUIDANCE AND COUNSELLING

Student ____

____

1. What evidence did you observe in your cooperating school of:

   (a) an effective programme for the selection and admission of students for the school?

   ____

   ____

   (b) an effective programme for counselling students for choice of occupation?

   ____

   ____

   (c) an effective programme for the placement and follow-up of students who have either dropped out or have completed the programme?

   ____

   ____

2. If there is not an adequate programme of guidance in the school, what steps is the school, considering in this direction?

____

____

3. Are adequate guidance-records maintained for students? Briefly describe the records used.

____

____

4. Comment on the extent of participation in the guidance-programme of the school by all members of the teaching staff.

____

____

5. Comment on the provisions for interviews with students who 'drop out' of the programme before completing it.

____

____

6. What suggestions would you make to improve the guidance service in any of its aspects?

____

____

ASSIGNMENT 15

COCURRICULAR ACTIVITIES

Student ____

1. What evidence did you observe that the administration of the school recognized the importance of cocurricular activities in the total school programme?

____

____

____

2. List the major cocurricular activities which you observed in operation in the school. Identify activities which you think ought to be added to the programme.

3. To what extent do all the students participate in some phase of the programme of cocurricular activities?

4. What are the measures adopted to provide cocurricular activities for all the students by the school?

5. What are the particular values of the cocurricular activities—programme of the school?

6. What use does the school make of community resources in order to carry out its cocurricular programme?

APPENDICES

APPENDIX-I

FORMAT FOR UNIT PLANNING

Title of the Unit :
Name of the Teacher :
School : Subject :
Class/Standard : Total Time :
Prerequisite Learning/Experiences:
Major objectives: (Concepts, Facts, Principles, Skills, Interest, etc.)

Sub Unit	Objectives/ Learning Outcomes	Content Analysis	Learning Activities/ Experiences	Evaluation Devices

APPENDIX-II

LESSON PLAN (SOCIAL SCIENCES) FORMAT

Date : Class & Section :
Topic :
Period : Duration :

A. General Aims
B. Specific Objectives/Behavioural
C. Teaching Aids/Teaching Materials
D. Teaching Methods
E. Previous Knowledge/Entering Behaviour
F. Introduction/Preparation/Motivation
G. Presentation

Teaching points	Teacher Activity	Pupil Activity

Blackboard Summary

H. Recapitulation/Evaluation
I. Assignment/Home work

APPENDIX-III

FORMAT (LANGUAGE TEACHING)

Lesson Plan No.

Date	:	Period	:
Subject	:	Unit	: (English Prose)
Topic	:		

A. General Aims
B. Specific Objectives/Behavioural
C. Teaching Aids/Teaching Materials
D. Teaching Methods
E. Previous Knowledge/Entering Behaviour
F. Introduction/Prepartion/Motivation
G. Teacher' Statement/Statement of Topic
H. Presentation
I. Model Reading
   (by the Teacher)
J. Loud Reading
   (2 or 3 students)
K. Pronunciation Drill
L. Vocab : Exposition
M. Phrases
N. Silent Reading
   (if necessary)
O. Comprehension Questions
P. Structures
Q. Grammatical points
   (if any)
R. Recapitulation/Evaluation
S. B.B. Summary (in points)
T. H.W./Class work

APPENDIX-IV

LESSON PLAN FORMAT (ENGLISH POETRY)

Lesson Plan No.

Date	:	Period	:
Subject	:	Unit	: (English Poetry)
Topic	:		

A. Ultimate/General Objectives :

(i) To Provide amusement and delight to the students by listening to poetry.

(ii) To develop their imaginative faculty and arousal of their emotions.

(iii) To create among the students love for English Language by feeling its rhyme and rhythm.

(iv) To train the students for appreciating English poetry.

(v) To inculcate among the students the aesthetic sense for different beauties in life.

B. Immediate (Behavioural) Objectives:

(Development of abilities related to Recitation, Comprehension, Appreciation, Critical Insight)

— To enable the students to recite the poem with proper rhyme and rhythm.

— To understand the content of the poem and to answer the questions based on the poem.

— To analyse the poem critically.

— To point out the different beauties of the poem.

C. Teaching-Learning Aids:

(i) Audio ....

(ii) Visual ....

(iii) Audio Visual ....

D. Method:

E. Preparation/Introduction/Motivation:

Through Audio-Visual Aids

— Similar poems

— Picturization etc.

Suspense and motivation be retained

F. Statement of the Aim/Topic
- — May be in a dramatic manner.
- — Writer's name only (Writer's introduction may be given after the presentation stage to form a better and clear image of the author)

G. Presentation

(i) Loud Reading (by the teacher)
- — with clear and correct pronunciation, necessary modulation.
- — recitation with the emphasis on stress, rhythm.
- — inculcate the total appreciation of the poem.

(ii) Loud Reading (by two or three students)

(This step may be taken up upto class VII. Generally loud reading is not required at the secondary stage.

(iii) Exposition :

Expression of words,
idioms and usage through various devices, techniques.

H. Recapitulation

I. B.B. Summary

APPENDIX-V

LESSON PLAN FORMAT (SCIENCE)

Lesson Plan No.

Date : Period : Time :

Class : Unit : Sec :

Subject : Topic/Title of the Lesson :

Objectives :

A. General (Only in 1st two lessons) :

B. Specific : Behavioural Objective (Specific to each topic)

Teaching-Learning Aids (i) Audio, (ii) Visual, (iii) Audio-Visual

Previous Knowledge (Entering Behaviour)

Introduction/Preparation/Motivation

Statement of Aim/Topic

Presentation

Class Room Interaction			
Teacher Point/ Content/Concept	Teacher-Activity	Pupil-Activity	Teacher Pupil Activity (in specific cases)

Blackboard work..

Recapitulation/Evaluation

Home Assignment/Excercise/Practice

APPENDIX-VI

हिन्दी शिक्षण 'गद्य'

पाठ योजना संख्या . . . .

दिनांक	:	कालांश	:
कक्षा	:	वर्ग	:
विषय	: हिन्दी	इकाई	: गद्य

उप इकाई/उप विषय 'पाठ' का नाम

उद्देश्य :

(अ) **सामान्य उद्देश्य :** सामान्य इकाई की पाठ योजनाओं के केवल प्रथम दो पाठ योजनाओं में शुद्ध उच्चारण, भाषा विकास सुनने, पढ़ने, समझने तथा बोलने की क्षमताओं के विकास सम्बन्धी नवीन शब्दों, कठिन शब्दों एवं व्याकरणिक तत्वों का बोध आदि।

(ब) **विशिष्ठ उद्देश्य/व्यावहारिक उद्देश्य :**
प्रत्येक पाठ के लिए विशिष्ठ उद्देश्यों अथवा ज्ञानात्मक, भावात्मक एवं मनोगामक 'कौशलात्मक' व्यावहारिक उद्देश्यों को लिखें।

अध्ययन – अध्यापन सामग्री :

पूर्वज्ञान :

प्रस्तावना/तैयारी/अभिप्रेरणा –

प्रश्नों के द्वारा, किसी संस्मरण द्वारा, प्रेरक पंक्तियों द्वारा, दृश्य-श्रव्य साधनों द्वारा आदि।

उद्देश्य कथन : उप विषय या पाठ के नाम एवं उसके लेखक के नाम की उद्‌घोषणा।

प्रस्तुतीकरण :

1. अध्यापक द्वारा गद्यखण्ड/पाठांश का आदर्श वाचन।
2. कतिपय विद्यार्थियों द्वारा अनुकरण वाचन।
3. काठिन्य निवारण : शब्द व्याख्या –

शब्द	अर्थ	विधि (व्याकरण द्वारा, विलोम, पर्यायवाची आदि के द्वारा)	प्रयोग

4. समस्त विद्यार्थियों से पाठांश का मौन वाचन।

श्यामपट्ट कार्य : कठिन शब्दों के अर्थ, लेखक का नाम शब्दों के वाक्य खण्ड एवं व्याकरणीकरण बातें आदि श्यामपट्ट पर लिखे जायेंगे।

बोध प्रश्न : पाठांश से सम्बन्धित उपलब्धियों की जांच हेतु लगभग पांच छः प्रश्न।

पुनरावृत्ति :

गृहकार्य/अभ्यास कार्य :

APPENDIX-VII

हिन्दी शिक्षण 'पद्य'

पाठ योजना संख्या . . . .

दिनांक	:	कालांश	:
कक्षा	:	वर्ग	:
विषय	: हिन्दी	इकाई	: कविता/गद्य

उद्देश्य :

(अ) **सामान्य उद्देश्य** : केवल प्रथम दो पाठ योजनाओं में उचित लय, आरोह-अवरोह एवं हाव-भाव के अनुसार कविता, सस्वर वाचन, रसानुभूति करना, कल्पना एवं सृजनात्मकता का विकास, भावनाओं का विकास आदि। रस, छंद एवं अलंकार का यथास्थान पहचान एवं प्रयोग।

(ब) **विशिष्ट उद्देश्य/व्यावहारिक उद्देश्य :**
प्रत्येक पद्य खण्ड/पाठांश के विशिष्ठ उद्देश्यों को स्पष्ट लिखें। यह भी स्पष्ट होना चाहिए कि प्रस्तुत पाठ/कविता से किस प्रकार के व्यवहार विद्यार्थियों में विकसित होंगे। भक्ति, राष्ट्रीय भावना, प्रकृति चित्रण, हास्य व्यंग्य आदि कविताओं के विशिष्ठ उद्देश्य अलग-अलग होंगे।

अध्ययन-अध्यापन सामग्री : दृश्य-श्रव्य सामग्री समान कविता, उपयुक्त चित्र, आदि।

पूर्वज्ञान :छात्रों की सम्बन्धित कविता/पद्य की पूर्व पीठिका या परिपेक्ष का संकेत।

प्रस्तावना/अभिप्रेरणा : समान भाव की कविता से रसानुभूति कराना, दृश्य-श्रव्य सामग्री के प्रयोग द्वारा।

उद्देश्य कथन : प्रस्तुत कविता एवं कवि के नामों की उद्घोषणा।

प्रस्तुतीकरण :

1. अध्यापक द्वारा पद्यांश का सरस्वर वाचन।
2. कतिपय विद्यार्थियों द्वारा अनुकरण वाचन।
3. काठिन्य निवारण : शब्द ज्ञान, समान सामग्री पंक्तियों द्वारा अथवा सीधे शब्दार्थ कथन द्वारा। अभिधा, लक्षणा एवं व्यंजना शब्द शक्तियों द्वारा

कविता की गूढ़ या अस्पष्ट भाव एवं कल्पना का स्पष्टीकरण।

4. मौन वाचन : कवि के भावों एवं अनुभूतियों को आत्मसात करने हेतु विद्यार्थियों द्वारा पद्यांश का मौन वाचन।

श्यामपट्ट कार्य : शब्दार्थ, कठिन अंशों की व्याख्या, भाव विश्लेषण सम्बन्धी कार्य जहां आवश्यक हो।

बोध प्रश्न : कविता के सौन्दर्य को स्पष्ट करने एवं विद्यार्थियों की उपलब्धियों की जांच हेतु लगभग पांच या छः प्रश्न। रस, छंद, अलंकार के पहचान एवं प्रयोग सम्बन्धी प्रश्न।

अभ्यास/गृहकार्य :

1. कुछ पंक्तियों की व्याख्या सम्बन्धी।
2. सृजनात्मकता के विकास हेतु कविता-सृजन का अभ्यास एवं पर्याप्त अभिप्रेरणा।
3. रस, छंद एवं अलंकार का समुचित प्रयोग।

APPENDIX-VIII

हिन्दी शिक्षण 'व्याकरण'

पाठ योजना संख्या . . . .

दिनांक	:	कालांश	:
कक्षा	:	वर्ग	:
विषय	: हिन्दी	इकाई	:

उपइकाई/उप विषय : व्याकरण के उस अंग का नाम जिसका अध्यापन आज किया जायगा।

उद्देश्य :

(अ) **सामान्य उद्देश्य** : केवल प्रथम दो पाठ योजनाओं में

- विभिन्न व्याकरणिक तत्वों का परिचय,
- नियम निर्धारण की योग्यता का विकास,
- व्याकरण के प्रभाव स्वरूप दैनिक जीवन में अनुशासन का विकास,
- भाषा की प्रकृति की समझ एवं भाषित तत्वों के समुचित प्रयोग की दक्षता का विकास
- अशुद्धियों (भाषा सम्बन्धी ज्ञान) के निराकरण के उपाय
- शब्द भण्डार की वृद्धि आदि।

(ब) **विशिष्ठ उद्देश्य/व्यावहारिक उद्देश्य** :

अध्ययन-अध्यापन सामग्री : चार्ट, श्रव्य-दृश्य सामग्री (आवश्यकतानुसार)

पूर्वज्ञान :

प्रस्तावना : वाक्य, शब्द एवं अनुच्छेद के उदाहरण एवं उन पर प्रश्न आदि।

उद्देश्य कथन : व्याकरणिक तत्व की उद्घोषणा करके।

प्रस्तुतीकरण :

–पढ़ाये जाने वाले व्याकरणिक अंग के अनेक उदाहरण दिये जायेंगे।

–उन उदाहरणों से सम्बन्धित प्रश्न पूछे जायेंगे। एवं उनका विश्लेषण एवं तुलना की जायेगी।

–नियम निर्धारण विद्यार्थियों की सहायता से।

–नियमीकरण में यथाअवसर अध्यापक द्वारा स्पष्टीकरण।

–निम्नलिखित रूपरेखा का उपयोग किया जा सकता है –

पाठ्य वस्तु उदाहरण	पाठ्य विधि विश्लेषण	श्यामपट्ट कार्य

सामान्यीकरण : विद्यार्थियों की सहायता से।

कक्षा-अभ्यास : प्रस्तुत व्यकरणिक अंग से सम्बन्धित नये उदाहरणों के अधार पर।

निरीक्षण : अध्यापक द्वारा।

गृहकार्य : पढ़ाये गये अंग से सम्बन्धित अभ्यास प्रश्न।

APPENDIX-IX

अन्तस्थ शिक्षण (INTERNSHIP IN TEACHING) योजनाबद्ध शिक्षण के उद्देश्य का लेखन

किसी भी कार्य की योजना अनेक स्तरों पर बनाई जाती है। शिक्षण योजना के भी कम से कम तीन स्तर हैं। पूरे वर्ष के पाठ्यक्रम की योजना, पाठ्यक्रम की प्रत्येक इकाई की योजना और इकाई के प्रत्येक पाठ की योजना।

योजना की सफलता प्रथमतः इस बात पर निर्भर होती है कि उसके उद्देश्य कितनी स्पष्टता से निर्धारित किए गए हैं। लम्बी अवधि की योजनाओं में उद्देश्य की दिशा निश्चित होनी चाहिए, मध्य-अवधि की योजनाओं (इकाई योजना) का स्तर स्पष्ट होना चाहिए और अल्प-अवधि की योजनाओं में उद्देश्य का रूप और आकार निश्चित होना चाहिए।

इकाई योजना मध्य-अवधि की शिक्षण योजना होती है इसलिए उसके उद्देश्यों का स्तर स्पष्ट होना चाहिए।

इन स्तरों में सम्मिलित हैं:

● ज्ञान (सूचना)।	Knowledge (Information)
● बोध (समझ)	Comprehension (Understanding)
● कौशल	Skill (of)
– अनुपयोग कौशल	— Application
– विशलेषण कौशल	— Analysis
– संश्लेषण कौशल	— Synthesis
– मूल्यांकन कौशल	— Evaluation
– क्रियात्मक कौशल	Psychomotor skills
● रुचि	Interest
● सराहना	Appreciation
● अभिवृत्ति	Attitude
● मूल्य	Values

उल्लेखनीय है कि सुविधा के लिए उपर्युक्त सूची में बौद्धिक कौशलों (अनुप्रयोगों, विश्लेषण) आदि और क्रियात्मक कौशल दोनों को इकट्ठे रखा गया है। चाहें तो उन्हें अलग-अलग श्रेणी मानकर भी लिखा जा सकता है।

पाठ योजना अल्प-अवधि की (30-35 मिनट के पाठ की) शिक्षण योजना होती है। इसका परिणाम तो कक्षा के तुरन्त बाद दिखाई दे देना चाहिए।

इसलिए पाठ योजना के उद्देश्य इतने स्पष्ट होने चाहिएं कि उनका रूप आसानी से पहचाना जा सके और परिणाम की जांच की जा सके। ऐसे उद्देश्यों में स्पष्ट रूप वाली क्रियाओं का उपयोग किया जाना चाहिए। सुविधा के लिए नीचे ऐसी क्रियाओं की एक सूची प्रस्तुत है जिनका प्रयोग उद्देश्यों के विभिन्न स्तरों पर किया जा सकता है।

ज्ञान-स्तर	*Knowledge Level*
पहचानना	Identify
नाम बताना	Name
नामांकित करना	Lable
पठन करना	Read/Decode
चुनना, छांटना	Select, Sort
मिलान करना	Match
सूची बनाना, गिनना	List
परिभाषा देना	Define
विवरण देना	State

बोध-स्तर	*Understanding Level*
रूपांतर करना, बदलना	Cover, Change
सरलार्थ करना	Paraphrase
नक्शा, ग्राफ आदि पढ़ना	Read (Map, graph etc.)
वर्गीकरण करना	Classify, Categories
क्रमबद्ध करना	Order Seriate
अन्तर स्पष्ट करना	Differentiate, Discriminate
तुलना करना	Compare
स्पष्ट करना	Explain
वर्णन करना	Describe
सारांश करना	Summaries
सम्बन्ध स्पष्ट करना	Relate
रूपरेखा बनाना	Outline
व्याख्या करना	Interpret
सिद्ध करना	Prove, Justify
विवेचना करना	Discuss
उदाहरण देना	Give Example, Illustrate

निष्कर्ष निकालना	Conclude
सामान्यीकरण करना	Generalise
संदेश, प्रवृति, मनोदशा आदि का अनुमान लगाना	Infer (message, trend, mood etc.)
भविष्य कथन करना	Predict

कौशल-स्तर

कौशल के स्तर पर क्रियाएं मुख्यतः वे ही होती हैं जो ऊपर सूचीबद्ध हैं। अन्तर यह है कि ज्ञान और बोध की क्रियाओं का उपयोग कौशल.स्तर के लिए सदैव नवीन सामग्री के साथ या नवीन स्थितियों में किया जाना चाहिये। यदि सामग्री और स्थिति वही रही तो कौशल का विकास संभव नही।

ऊपर इकाई योजना के अन्तर्गत कौशल में विभिन्न प्रकारों का उल्लेख किया जा चुका है। उनमें अनुप्रयोग.कौशल विभिन्न विषयों में अलग प्रकार के होते हैं यथा :

अनुप्रयोग-कौशल

गणित में	–	जोड़ना, घटाना, हल करना, गणना करना आदि। Add, Subtract, Solve, Compute etc.
भाषा	–	पठन, वाचन वाक्य-प्रयोग, वाक्य विश्लेषण, पद परिचय आदि। Read, Recite, Use in Sentence, Analyse, Sentence, Phrase etc.
विज्ञान में	–	हल करना, समीकरण संतुलित करना आदि। Solve, Numerial Balance Equation etc.
वाणिज्य में	–	प्रविष्ट करना आदि।

इनके अतिरिक्त प्रत्येक विषय में ज्ञान और बोध की क्रियाओं की नई स्थिति में करें तो कौशल होगा ही।

विष्लेषण-कौशल

नई सामग्री के साथ/With New Material

ज्ञानात्मक क्रिया – पहचानना, चुनना, सूचीबद्ध करना।
Identify, Select, List,

बोधात्मक क्रियाएं – वर्गीकरण करना, अन्तर स्पष्ट करना, संबंध स्पष्ट करना, रूपरेखा बनाना, स्पष्ट करना, निष्कर्ष निकालना।
Classify, Distinguish, Relate, Outline, Explain, Conclude etc.

अन्य – खण्डित करना, अलग करना, उपविभाजित करना आदि।
Breakdown, Separate, Subdivide etc.

नई सामग्री के साथ नये रूप में

ज्ञानात्मक क्रियाएं – परिभाषा देना, Define

बोधात्मक क्रियाए – बदलना, वर्गीकरण करना, क्रमबद्ध करना, वर्णन करना, रूपरेखा बनाना, सिद्ध करना आदि।
Convert, Classity, Order, Describe, Outline, Prove etc.

अन्य – रचना, योजना बनाना, डिज़ाइन बनाना, सुधारना, कविता आदि लिखना।
Compose, Plan, Design, Modify, Write Poem etc.

नई सामग्री के साथ

आलोचनात्मक रूप से, तुलना करना, अन्तर स्पष्ट करना, विवेचना करना, मूल्यांकन करना, समीक्षा करना, सीमांश करना आदि।
Critically compare distinguish, discuss, evaluate, appraise assess etc.

क्रियात्मक कौशल

कोण, ग्राफ, नक्शा आदि बनाना	Draw angle, graph, map etc
रंग भरना	Colour, paint
नापना	Measure
उपकरण व्यवस्थित करना	Set apparatus
सराहना	Write (neatly)

'सराहना' मूलतः अनुभूति पर अधारित होती है और बौद्धिक समझ के बिना भी संभव है किंतु उसकी क्रियाओं का स्वरूप 'बोध' का ही होता है। 'सरहाना' की प्रमुख क्रियाएं हैं–

सराहनीय बिन्दु/तत्व/को/की	
चुनाव/छांटना	Select
इंगित करना	Point out
स्पष्ट करना	Explain
व्याख्या करना	Interpret
उदाहरण द्वारा पुष्टि करना	Support (with example) etc.
	appreciable point

रुचि अभिवृत्ति, मूल्य पूर्णरूप में भावपूर्वक उद्देश्य है और उनको व्यवहारिक रूप में देखा जा सकता है। लिखित स्वरूप में इन उद्देश्यों को नहीं बांधा जा सकता।

"स्वेच्छापूर्वक कार्य करना" "खोजना" "एकत्र करना" आदि रुचि के स्वरूप हैं। पहल करना समर्थन करना तर्क सिद्ध करना अनुगमन करना आदि

अभिवृत्ति उद्देश्यों का स्वरूप हैं ये ही परिपक्व होकर मूल्य-स्तर पर पहुंच जाते हैं। इन स्तरों के उद्देश्य दीर्घ-अवधि या मध्यवर्ती-अवधि के अधिक उपयुक्त हैं, दैनिक पाठ-योजना के लिए उतने संभव नहीं होते।

APPENDIX-X

SUPERVISION OF LESSON

Name of the Teacher Training Institution..

Lesson No..............................

Date.......................... Subject....................... Class & Section...........

Period....................... Unit.......................... Topic.........................

Teacher Trainee's (Intern) Name...

Class.......................... Enrolment No..

Aspects : Criteria	*Comments and Suggestions*
1. *Lesson Plan* : (Objectives and Content, Adequacy, Accuracy, Clarity, Organisation, Appropriateness, Writing, Attractiveness, Expression)	
2. *Introduction/Motivation/Preparation/ Set Induction* Use of entering behaviour, Initiative and imagination, Interest, Questioning and other devices	
3. *Presentation* Content-Command, Accuracy, Technique, Strategies, Methods, Sequential Steps, Appropriateness, Reinforcement and Feedback.	
A. *Communication* : Questioning, Language, Fluency, Speed, Pronunciation, Tone, Clarity of Voice, Non-verbal communication, Interaction, Intonation, Pauses, Movements, Gesture, Expression	
B. *Teaching Learning Process:* Classroom Activities, Experiments,	

Demonstration etc.

C. *Teaching Learning Material/ Teaching Aids (including Blackboard work)*:
Management, Appropriateness, Adequacy, Effectiveness, Originality, Variety, Computation, Attractiveness.

4. *Class Management*
Arrangement and Organization of Material, Space Management, Discipline, Learning, climate, Class control, Time Management

5. *Closure*
Evaluation/Review/Recapitulation, Assignments

6. *Personality*
Self Confidence, Professional Zeal, Expression, Rapport with Students, Punctuality and Sincerity, Manners

7. *Ranking*

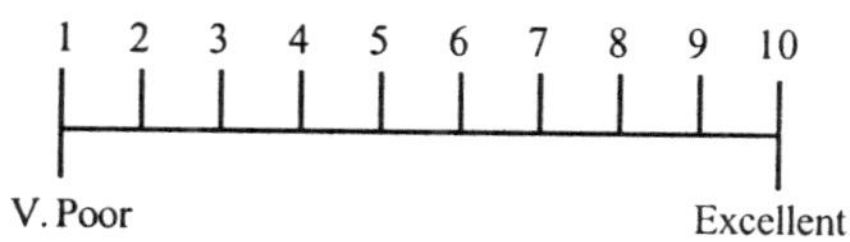

Signature of the Supervisor

APPENDIX-XI

TOOL FOR EVALUATION - I
CORE - TRAINING

MM 20%

1. *Skill of Motivation/Preparation :*
    1. Stimulating
    2. Arousing curosity
    3. Creating interest
    4. Focusing attention

2. *Presentation :*
    1. Sequencial
    2. Effective
    3. Interesting
    4. Understandable

3. *Skill of Questioning* :
    1. To the point
    2. Probing
    3. Precision
    4. Correctness

4. *Skill of Explanation :*
    1. Logicality
    2. Language
    3. Illustrations
    4. Expression

5. *Blackboard Work :*
    1. Neatness
    2. Writing
    3. Systematic
    4. Precision

APPENDIX-XII

TOOL FOR EVALUATION - II
REGULAR LESSONS

MM 20%

1. Lesson Planning
2. Introducing/Motivation/Preparation
3. Presentation
4. Content-grasp
5. Communication
6. Teacher Pupil Interaction
7. Teaching Aids
8. Blackboard Work
9. Class Management
10. Personality

APPENDIX-XIII-A

EVALUATION IN INTERNSHIP
DISTRIBUTION OF MARKS

			Marks
1.	Core-Training		20%
2.	Regular Lessons		20%
3.	Criticism Lesson		10%
	Subject I	5%	
	Subject II	5%	
4.	Final Lesson		20%
	Subject I	10%	
	Subject II	10%	
5.	Assignment Subject I		5%
6.	Assignment Subject II		5%
7.	Edn. Assignment		5%
8.	Principal/Teacher of Co-operating Schools		5%
9.	Peer evaluators		5%
10.	Self evaluation		5%

APPENDIX-XIII

TOOL FOR EVALUATION - III & IV

Criticism Lesson MM 10%

I Subjet 5%

II Subjet 5%

Final Lessons MM 20%

I Subjet 5%

II Subjet 5%

Points for Evaluation	*Criticism Lesson*		*Final Lesson*	
	I Subject 5%	*II Subject 5%*	*I Subject 10%*	*II Subject 10%*
1. Lesson Planning				
2. Introduction/Motivation/ Preparation				
3. Presentation				
4. Content-grasp				
5. Communication				
6. Teacher Pupil Interaction				
7. Teaching Aids				
8. Blackboard Work				
9. Class Management				
10. Personality				

APPENDIX-XIV

TOOL FOR EVALUATION — V, VI AND VIII ASSIGNMENT SUBJECT I, II AND EDUCATION

MM 5% + 5% + 5%

1. Data Collection
2. Relevance
3. Sincerity
4. Presentation
5. Resourcefulness

APPENDIX-XV

TOOL FOR EVALUATION — VIII PRINCIPALS/TEACHERS OF COOPERATING SCHOOLS

5%

1. Sincerity
2. Punctuality
3. Initiative
4. Co-operations Obedience
5. Discipline

APPENDIX-XVI

TOOL FOR EVALUATION — IX
INTERNSHIP IN TEACHING
LESSON OBSERVATION SCHEDULE

Date.......................... Subject........................ Class & Section...........

Period........................ Unit........................... Topic............................

Teacher Trainee's (Intern) name...

Direction : Observe and comment on the various aspects on criteria as mentioned in the schedule

Aspects : Criteria	*Comments and Suggestions*	*Rating*
1. *Lesson Plan* : (Objectives and Contents, Adequacy, Accuracy, Clarity, Organisation, Writing and Expression, Delivery)		Excellent 5 4 3 2 1 Poor
2. *Introduction/Motivation/Preparation:* (Technique, Use of previous knowledge, Imagination, Originality, Interest, Aids and Approach.		Excellent 5 4 3 2 1 Poor
3. *Presentation* Questioning, Explanation Exposition, Examples, Illustrations, Analogy, Discussions, Demonstration, Concept Formation and Generalization, Promotion of Critical Thinking, Sequential Steps, Teacher Pupil Interaction Content : Accuracy, Adequacy, Command, Clarity, Time Management		Excellent 5 4 3 2 1 Poor

	Aspects : Criteria	Comments and Suggestions	Rating
4.	*Teacher-Learning Material Management:* Appropriateness, Adequacy, Effectiveness, Variety, Computation, Quality Technical Skill, Relevance, Use of Artifacts.		Excellent 5 4 3 2 1 Poor
5.	*Class-Management:* Congenial Learning Climate, Discipline, Space Management, Class control, Interaction, Degree of classroom participation by most of the student's		Excellent 5 4 3 2 1 Poor
6.	*Use of Blackboard:* Clearness, Explicit, Economy, Appropriateness, Writing, Lettering, Spacing, Uniformity, Organisation, Spellings, Drawing, Student's Involvement.		Excellent 5 4 3 2 1 Poor
7.	*Teacher's Personality:* Confidence, Professional Zeal, Communication Skill, Rapport with Students, Punctuality and Sincerety, Movement, Mannerism, Dress, Language, Voice, Modulation, Pronunciation, Fluency, Scholarship, Expression, Vitality, Originality.		Excellent 5 4 3 2 1 Poor
8.	*Closure:* Evaluation/Review/Recapitulation, Assignments, Coverage, Home work (Type, Utility).		Excellent 5 4 3 2 1 Poor

APPENDIX-XVII

TOOL FOR EVALUATION — X
SELF EVALUATION

MM. 5%

1. Honesty
2. Teaching Aptitude
3. Objectivity
4. Sincerity
5. Dutifulness

APPENDIX-XVIII

STUDENT-TEACHER'S DIARY

(To be submitted immediately after returning from Internship Centre)

1. Name:

2. Centre:

3. School:

4. No. of lessons observed by :
   (a) the College Supervisors
   (b) the Cooperating Teacher

	Method I	Method II	Total
Total			

5. Total No. of lessons given by the Student teacher :

6. Details of the lessons given :

S. No.	Date	Period	Class	Sub./ Topic	Evaluated by (with teacher's name)	Remarks

7. Details of the lessons observed by the Student Teacher

S. No.	Date	Period	Class	Sub./ Topic	Name of the Teacher	Remarks

8. Total No. of lessons observed:

Subjects	Methods I	Methods II	Total
No. of Lessons			

9. Details of tests conducted by the student teacher :

S. No.	Date	Class	Period	Sub./ Topic	Total No. of Tests

10. Co-curricular activities organized/participated :

APPENDIX-XIX

THE ROLE OF AUDIO-VISUAL AIDS

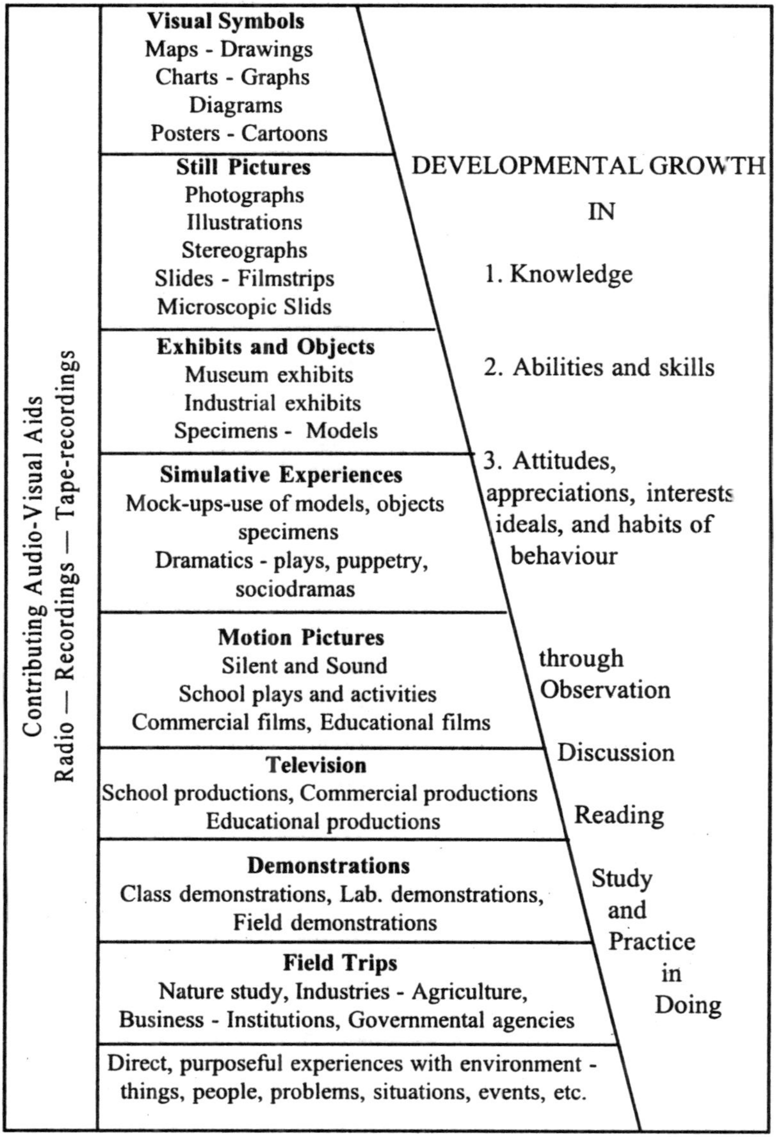

APPENDIX-XX

ENHANCING LEARNING

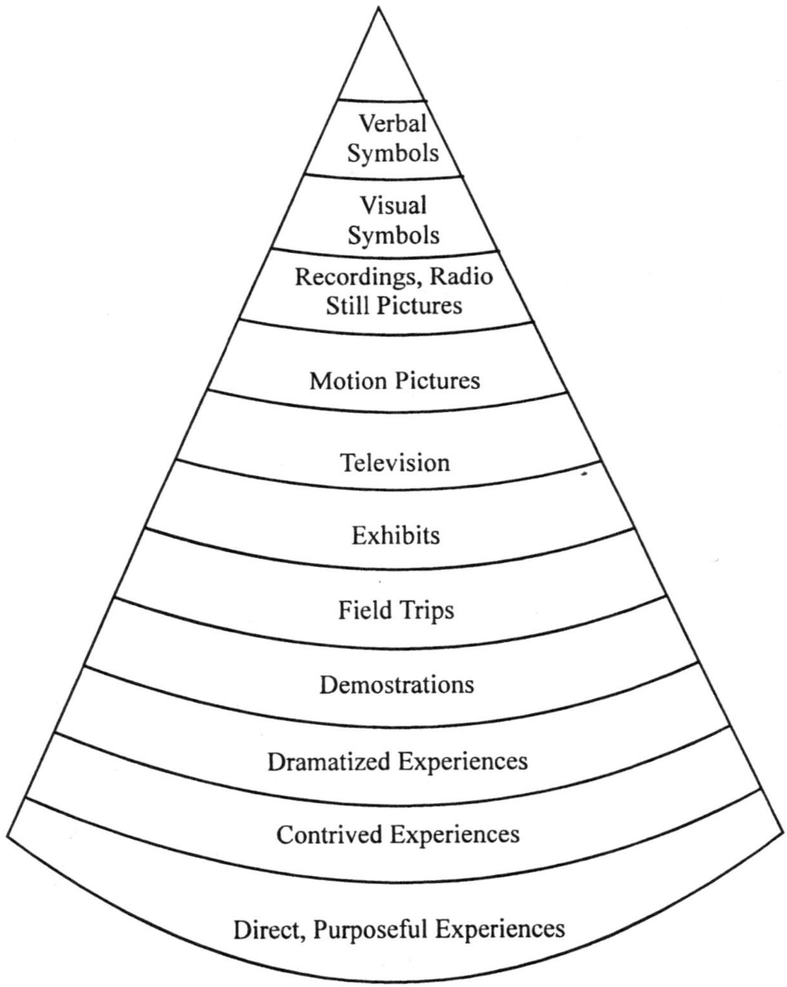

APPENDIX-XXI

STUDENT-TEACHER'S SELF-EVALUATION SHEET

Name :

School :

Date :

1. To what extent was your planning adequate for the class teaching?

____

____

____

2. How often have you revised a lesson plan after discussion with the cooperating teacher?

   Frequently : ______________________________

   Occasionally : ______________________________

   Never : ______________________________

3. List the teaching aids you prepared during your teaching :

____

____

____

4. Mention any aids other than charts or maps which you used :

____

____

____

5. How many of these did you prepare yourself?

____

6. What resource books did you find helpful in planning for the units you taught

____

____

7. Did you supplement the textbook material? If so, by what means?

____

____

____

8. What is the extent of student response to home assignments?

____

____

9. Is the nature of assignments you gave to students varied from time to time? If so, how did you make provision for this?

____

____

10. How frequently did you have to reward a question in the class?
    Frequently : ______________________________

    Occasionally : ______________________________

    Never : ______________________________

11. In how many lessons did you utilize the following techniques?
    1. Teacher-pupil planning : ______________________________
    2. Group assignments : ______________________________
    3. Supervised study : ______________________________
    4. Demonstration : ______________________________
    5. Problem approach : ______________________________
    6. Other : ______________________________

12. How many discipline cases did you handle?

____

____

In how many were you successfull?
(Give the specific nature of the cases handled)

BIBLIOGRAPHY

Bawa, M.S. (1984). Effectiveness of Micro Teaching with Planned Integration Training, Following Summative Model of Micro Teaching Without Planned Integration Training on the General Teaching Competence of Teacher Trainees. Ph.D. Edu. Delhi University.

Bellack, A.A., Kliebard, H.M., Hyman, R.T. and Smith, F.L. (1966). *The Language of the Classroom*. Teachers College Press, New York.

Bennie, William A. (1972). *Supervising Clinical Experiences in the Classroom*. Harper & Row, New York.

Bhatnagar, T.N.S. (1980). Studies and Literature on Student Teaching and other Practical Work in the B.Ed. Programme in India—Review. Deptt. of Teacher Ed. Project NCERT, New Delhi.

Bhatt, M.M. (1966). *Kapasan Scheme of Improvement in Teacher Training*. SIERT Rajasthan.

Bhattacharjee, (1981). *Effectiveness of Micro Teaching in Developing Teaching Competence*. Extension Service Deptt. Post Graduate Training College, Shillong.

Bloom, B.S. (Ed.), Engethart, M.D., Furst, E.J., Hill, W.H. and Krathwohl, D.R. (1956). *Taxonomy of Educational Objectives: The Classification of Educational Goals, Handbook I :* The Cognitive Domain. Longmans Green, New York.

Bloom, B.S. (Ed.), (1956). *Taxonomy of Educational Objectives : Cognitive Domain*. New York : David Mekay.

Buch, M.B. (Ed.) (1974). *A Survey of Research in Education*. CASE, Baroda.

Buch, M.B. (Ed.) (1979). *Second Survey of Research in Education*. Soc. Edl. Res. & Dev., Baroda.

Buch, M.B. (Chief Ed.) (1986). *Third Survey of Research in Education*. NCERT, New Delhi.

Buch, M.B. (Chief Ed.) (1991). *Fourth Survey of Research in Education*. NCERT, New Delhi.

Callahan, Sterling, G. (1966). *Successful Teaching in Secondary Schools*. Scott Foresman and Company, Grenview, Illinois.

Chathley, (1984). An Experimental Study of the Teaching Competency at Macro-level as a Function of Training in Micro Skills Among the Prospective Secondary School Teachers in Relation to the Integration of Skills and Subject Area, Ph.D. Ed. Pan University.

Cicirelli, V.G. (1969). University Supervisors' Creative Ability and Their Appraisal of Student Teachers' Performance. An Exploratory Study. *Jr. Edu. Res.* 62.

Clarke, S.C.T. (1970). 'General Teaching Theory'. *Jr. Teach. Ed.* 21, 3.

Cope, E. (1971). *School Experience in Teacher Education. Research Unit.* School of Education, Bristol University.

Cruz, Leonardo de la (1988). Development and Reform in Teacher Education. *Bulletin of the UNESCO* : PROAP. No. 29.

Das, R.C., Passi, B.K. and Singh, L.C. (1976). *A Study of the Effectiveness of Micro-teaching in the Training of Teacher*, NCERT (New Delhi) and CASE Baroda.

Deo, D.S. (1985). To Study the Practical Programme other than Practice Teaching in Teacher Education Institutions. Ph.D. Education, Delhi University.

Dholakia, J.V. (1980), Effects of Observers and Feedback Upon Changing the Classroom Performance of Pupil-Teacher, Ph.D. Edu., M.S. University.

Donald, R. Cruickshand and Frank W. Broadbent (1970). *Simulation in Preparing School Personnel.* ERIC Clearinghouse on Teacher Education, Washington, D.C.

Dorothy, S. Blackmore. (1968). "Integration of Theory and Practice in Internship". Internships in Teacher Education. Association for Student Teaching, *47th Yearbook*, Washington, D.C.

Dwight, Allen. W. (1994). *An update on Micro-teaching Formats*. Old Dominion University. Norfolk. VA 23529.

Dwight, K. Curtis, (Ed.) (1957). *Achieving Quality in Off-Campus Professional Laboratory Experiences Bulletin No. 8*. Association for Student Teaching, Washington, D.C.

EdCIL, (1987). *Programme of Improvement of Secondary Teacher Education Institutions,* Educational Consultants India Ltd., New Delhi.

Ekbote, E.R. (1987). Development of a Strategy for Integration of Skills in Teacher Training. Ph.D. Education. MS University.

Flanders, N. (1961). Interaction Analysis: A Technique for Quantifying Teacher Influence. Paper Presented to the A.E.R.A. (mimeo).

Gupta, Arun K. Zadoo, C.K. Bhan, I., Tikku, K. Balia, J.N. (1992). The

Impact of Teaching Kit on the Trainees: An Evaluative Study. *Jr. Ind. Edu.* Vol. 16, No. 5.

Gupta, R.P. (1979) A Study of Some Factors Considered to be Helpful in Class Teaching. Ph.D. Edu. Lucknow University.

Gupta, V.P., Sindhu, R.S., Gupta, S.K., Sharma, R., and Khan, Z.A. (1995). Documentation of In-service Teachers Training Practices in Western Region of India. R.I.E. (NCERT) Bhopal.

Harrow, A.J. (1972). Hwarrow, A.J. (1972). *A Taxonomy of Psychomotor Domain*. New York: Davide Mekay.

Hillard, Pauline and Charles, L. Durrance (1968). Guiding Student Teaching Experiences, *Bulletin No. 1*. Rev. Association for Student Teaching. Washington, D.C.

Hoover, Kenneth H. (1964). *Learning and Teaching in the Secondary School.* Allyn and Bacon, Inc. Boston.

John. G. Chaltas *et al.* (1968). "The Supervision of Intern Teachers," Internship in Teacher Education. Association for Student Teaching. *47th Yearbook*, Washington, D.C.

Joshi, D.C. (1972). *A Study of Innovations and Changes in Teachers Colleges.* Ph.D. Education. Udaipur University (Vol. 1).

Joyce, B. and Weil, Marsha (1980). *Models of Teaching.* Prentice-Hall, Inc. Englewood Cliffs. New Jersey.

Kestner, James L. (1994). *New Teacher Induction : Findings of the Research and Implications for Minority Groups Jr. Teacher Edu.* Vol. 45 No. 1.

Kounin, J.S. (1970). *Discipline and Group Management in Classrooms.* New York : Holt, Rinehart & Winston, New York.

Krathwohl, D.R. Bloom, B.S. and Masis, B.B. (1964). *Taxonomy of Educational Objectives : Affective Domain.* New York : David Mekay.

McGreal, T.L. (1983). *Successful Teacher Evaluation. VA : Association for Supervision and Curriculum Development Alexandria.*

Medical Council of India (1983). *Recommendations on Graduate Medical Education.* Published and Sold by The Medical Council of India.

M.H.R.D. Govt. of India (1986). *National Policy on Education.* New Delhi.

M.H.R.D. Govt. of India (1992). *Programme of Action.* New Delhi.

Mohanty, S.B. (1984). A Study of Student Teaching Programmes in Colleges of Education with Special Reference to Innovation, Ph.D. Edu. M.S. University.

Mukhopadhyay, M. *et al.* (1981). *An Action Research on Alternative Models of Teacher Training*, TTTI, Bhopal.

Natrajan, S.A., (1984). *A Competency Based Programme in Teacher Education Curriculum*, Ph. D. Edu., Madras University.

N.C.E.R.T. (1963). *Plan and Programme*. NCERT New Delhi.

N.C.E.R.T. (1964). *Internship in Teaching*. NCERT, New Delhi.

N.C.E.R.T. (1978). *Teacher Education Curriculum*. NCERT, New Delhi.

N.C.E.R.T. (1979). *Organisation of Core Training Programme Package*. NCERT, New Delhi.

N.C.E.R.T. (1988). *National Curriculum for Teacher Education,* Deptt. of Teacher Ed., Special Ed. and Ext. Services NCERT, New Delhi.

N.C.E.R.T. (1991). *Secondary Teacher Edu. Curriculum Guidelines and Syllabi*. NCERT, New Delhi.

Oak, A.W., (1986). A Critical Study of Microteaching Techniques With a View to Suggest Improvement in its Implementation in Colleges of Education. Deptt. of P.G. Edu. and Res., SNDT University.

Pande, S.M. (1980). *A Critical Study of Supervision Practices*, Ph.D. Edu. Avadh University.

Passi, B.K. (Ed.) (1976). *Becoming Better Teacher*. Sahitya Maudranalaya. Ahmedabad.

Passi, B.K. and Sharma, S.K. (1982). *A Study of Teaching Competency of Secondary School Teachers*. Deptt. of Edu., Indore University.

Passi, B.K., Singh, L.C., and Sansanwal, D.N. (1986). Implementing Training Strategies and Studying Effectiveness of Different Variations in Components of Training Strategy for Concept Attainment Model/ Inquiry/Training Model in Terms of Understanding, Competency, Reactions and Willingness of Student Teachers. Deptt. of Edu. Davv.

Raina, V.K. (1995). Teacher Education in India : In Search of an Identity. *Jr. Teacher Education*. Vol. 46. No. 1.

Ralph, Edwin G. (1994). Helping Beginning Teachers Improve Via Contextual Supervision. *Jr. Teacher Edu.* Vol. 45. No. 5.

R.I.E. (1995). Supervisor's Diary, Guideline for Internship Programme, Internship Supervision, Internship in Teaching (Micro Teaching), Lesson Observation Schedule, Lesson Notes, Supervision Notebook. R.I.E. Bhopal.

Risk, Thomas M. (1965). *Principles and Practices of Teaching in Secondary Schools*. Eurasia Publishing House (Pvt.) Ltd. Ram Nagar, New Delhi.

Rosenshine, Barak (1995). Advances in Research on Instruction. *Jr. Educ. Res.* Vol. 88 No. 5.

Shah, M.M. (1986). *A Survey of Management of Student Teaching in India.* CASE, M.S. University.

Sharma, R.A. (1986). *Technology of Teaching.* Loyal Book Depot. Meerut.

Sharma, Y.K. and Kumar, N. (1983). Relative Importance of Teaching Skills : Views of Secondary Schools Teachers. *Jr. Ind. Ed.* Vol. 18, No. 6.

Singh, L.C. (1982). *Third National Survey of Secondary Teacher Education in India.* NCERT, New Delhi.

Singh, N. (1985). *A Comparative Study of Teachers Trained Through Integrated and Traditional Methods in Terms of Attitude Towards Teaching, Teaching Competance and Role Performance*, Ph.D. Edu., B.H. University (B.H.U.).

Singh, Satyanarayan (1984). *Effect of Training in Teaching Skills Using Micro-Class, Peers and Real Pupils on the General Teaching Competence of Student Teachers.* DSERT, Karnataka.

Stones, E. and Morris, S. (1972). *Teaching Practice : Problems and Perspectives.* Methuen & Co. Ltd., London.

Strawderman, Carol and Lindsey, Pamela (1995). Keeping up With the Times : Reform in Teacher Education. *Jr. Teacher Edu.* Vol. 46. No. 2.

Srivastava, G.N.P. *et al.* (1996). *A Study of Internship in Teaching With a View to Develop Strategies for its Improvement.* R.I.E. (NCERT), Bhopal.

Switzer, R. (1976). Cooperating Teachers' Strengths and Weaknesses. *J. Edu. Res.* 15.

Teprongtong, S. (1984). *Role Expectations and the Role Performance of College Supervisors on Student Teaching as Perceived by School Principals,* Cooperating Teachers and Student Teachers Ph.D. Edu., Pan. University

Tulley, Michael & Chiu, Lian Hawang (1995). Student Teachers and Classroom Discipline. *Jr. Educ. Res.* Vol. 88, No. 3.

Van Antwerp, Chiles (1964). *Student Teaching at Peabody.* George Peabody College for Teachers.

Index